A Depth Psychological Study of the Peace Symbol

This engaging new book uncovers the cultural context behind the peace symbol's emergence, its growing significance in the 1960s, and its ongoing presence in today's worldwide grassroots and non-violent social action protests.

Since its debut in 1958, the peace symbol has become a ubiquitous presence in broadcasted images of protest and resistance, yet most citizens are unaware of the symbol's history or psychological evolution. It is a unique modern symbol in that it is at once an omnipresent and yet entirely unknown entity. This noteworthy text engages readers in fresh and thought-provoking ways around the interdependent relationships of peace and war, recognition and secrets, symbol and chaos, and action and inaction to name a few. In this book, Rivera-Clonch brings a depth psychological analysis to Post-World War II's escalating nuclear tensions and rhetoric and links it to today's increasing consciousness around social injustices and nonviolent activism. This is a timely and relevant interdisciplinary case study exploring the peace symbol through the dimensions of cultural secrets and psychological shadow, nuclearized storytelling and symbology, and grassroots nonviolent social action.

A Depth Psychological Study of the Peace Symbol will be of interest to Jungian and depth psychologists, as well as students and scholars of peace studies and psychology.

Michelle Rivera-Clonch, PhD, is a depth psychologist and licensed mental health counselor in private practice. She additionally works as a peace-based international scholar-practitioner, teaches undergraduate and graduate students, and is a co-founder of an annual academic writing retreat for faculty in higher education—WritinginDepth.org.

Routledge Focus on Jung, Politics and Culture

The Jung, Politics and Culture series showcases the 'political turn' in Jungian and Post-Jungian psychology. Established and emerging authors offer unique perspectives and new insights as they explore the connections between Jungian psychology and key topics–including national and international politics, gender, race and human rights.

For a full list of titles in this series, please visit https://www.routledge.com/Focus-on-Jung-Politics-and-Culture/book-series/FJPC

Titles in the series:

Torture Survivors in Analytical Therapy: Jung, Politics and Culture
Monica Luci

Racial Legacies: Jung, Politics and Culture
Fanny Brewster & Helen Morgan

From Vision to Folly in the American Soul: Jung, Politics and Culture
Thomas Singer

Vision, Reality and Complex: Jung, Politics and Culture
Thomas Singer

Anti-Semitism and Analytical Psychology: Jung, Politics and Culture
Daniel Burston

A Depth Psychological Study of the Peace Symbol
Jung, Politics, and Culture

Michelle Rivera-Clonch

LONDON AND NEW YORK

First published 2024
by Routledge
4 Park Square, Milton Park, Abingdon, Oxon OX14 4RN

and by Routledge
605 Third Avenue, New York, NY 10158

Routledge is an imprint of the Taylor & Francis Group, an informa business

© 2024 Michelle Rivera-Clonch

The right of Michelle Rivera-Clonch to be identified as author of this work has been asserted in accordance with sections 77 and 78 of the Copyright, Designs and Patents Act 1988.

All rights reserved. No part of this book may be reprinted or reproduced or utilised in any form or by any electronic, mechanical, or other means, now known or hereafter invented, including photocopying and recording, or in any information storage or retrieval system, without permission in writing from the publishers.

Trademark notice: Product or corporate names may be trademarks or registered trademarks, and are used only for identification and explanation without intent to infringe.

British Library Cataloguing-in-Publication Data
A catalogue record for this book is available from the British Library

ISBN: 978-1-032-46464-0 (hbk)
ISBN: 978-1-032-46463-3 (pbk)
ISBN: 978-1-003-38179-2 (ebk)

DOI: 10.4324/b23325

Typeset in Times New Roman
by Newgen Publishing UK

To the Ancestors...and with radical optimism for our descendants.

Contents

Acknowledgments   *ix*
List of Acronyms   *xi*

Introduction   1

PART I
Shadow: Cultural Secret Detonated   12
   Psychological Shadow 12
   Cultural Secret: The Manhattan Project 15
   Mythology Aplenty: Archetypal Frontier, Apocalypse,
     Modern-Day Alchemy and Pygmalion 18
   Ego and Shadow Tarry Together 23
   Cultural Secret Detonated 26

PART II
Enantiodromia: RadioActive Psyche   32
   Psychological Enantiodromia 32
   The Atomic Age Opens 35
   Modern Day Prometheus? 37
   Nuclear Paranoia and Fallout 39
   RadioActive Psyche: Duck and Cover, Godzilla, *UFOs,*
     and Fallout Shelters 41

PART III
Symbol: "A Human Being in Despair" — 52
Britain's Own Little Secret Leads to the Era of Mass Protests 53
"A Human Being in Despair" 57
To Be or Not to Be? 63
Symbolic Form Against Psychological Chaos 67
Something Dynamic Happened 73

PART IV
Kairos: Alchemizing the Golden Shadow — 81
There's Gold in the British Shadow 82
Alchemizing the Golden Shadow 85
Kairos—The Right Time, Place, and People 89
Doing Nothing Sets It Free 90
The Peace Symbol Immigrates to the U.S. 96

Conclusion: Today's Relevance — 118

Index — 128

Acknowledgments

Contrary to the belief that academic writing is the product of a single author's divine inspiration, my experience is that it is the manifestation of a large community of people, fellow writers, and non-writers, who contribute in discreet and important ways out of love, collegiality, support, expertise, random acts of kindness, and with appeal to humanity's better angels. I experienced an incredible level of support from these varied circles of community.

My deepest gratitude extends to each of you for your part in this project over the past year.

To the Abiding Constants: My beloved parents—Dan and Maria Clonch; my Love—Ivan Aguigui Jr.; my girls—Molly the Boston Terrier and Crinkle the Toy Poodle; and my indefatigable HH Crew in alphabetical order—Natasha Arnold, Mikel Awad, Melissa Cavida, Sharen Keomany, and Eddie Perez.

To The Experts: At Routledge—Editor Katie Randall who took a chance on me and the subject matter; Editorial Assistant and gem Alice Maher who kept the process moving smoothly, and Senior Editor Neil Jordan who first fielded my proposal and gave it a go. The folks at NewGen who gave their much needed eagle-eyed expertise. At the Swarthmore College Peace Collection—Grace Diliberto, Anne Yoder, Mary Beth Sigado, David Obermayer, Rachel Mattson, James Truitt, Caitlynn Goodman, and Victoria Russo. At the University of Bradford—Julie Parry. The staff at the Campaign for Nuclear Disarmament and at Peace News—Milan Rai and Emma Sangster. Dr. Kathryn Norsworthy and Dr. Jennifer Selig who were irreplaceable at this project's origin. Matthew Clonch for his graphic design expertise, and to the anonymous external reviewers who gave feedback that supported the publication of this book.

To The Inspiring: Those who have passed on—Peggy Duff, Thich Nhat Hanh, Thomas Merton, the founding leaders of the CND, SPU, CNVA and Peace News, Paulo Freire, Ignacio Martin-Baro, and Zora Neale Hurston. And those I am supremely blessed to know—Kathryn Norsworthy, Sor Isabel Rivera-Feliciano, Alexandra Merrill, Suzanne Stevens, and Ouyporn Khuenkaew.

To The Serendipitous and Kind Hearted: Years and years of colleagues at *Writing in Depth: An Academic Writing Retreat* (WritingInDepth.org); colleagues and friends at Hope Springs Institute, family and friends who were patient as I declined invitation after invitation to focus on the writing, colleagues and clients from my private practice (PeaceWithinCounseling.com) who offered words of encouragement and support when they learned of my project, and Nikki Dennis who held it all together.

Acronyms

AEC	Atomic Energy Commission (United States) (U.S.)
AWE	Atomic Weapons Establishment (Great Britain) (GB)
CND	Campaign for Nuclear Disarmament (GB)
CNVA	Committee for Nonviolent Action (U.S.)
DAC	Direct Action Committee Against Nuclear War (GB)
FCDA	Federal Civil Defense Administration (U.S.)
MED	Manhattan Engineer District (U.S.)
ND	Nuclear Disarmament
OED	Oxford English Dictionary
SANE	National Committee for a Sane Nuclear Policy (U.S.)
SPU	Student Peace Union (U.S.)
UND	Unilateral Nuclear Disarmament

Introduction

If you picked up this book and are reading this introduction, I am willing to bet that you, too, are intrigued by the peace symbol, the circle containing two lines—one line extending north to south down the center, the other a north pointing chevron starting at 4 o'clock on the face of a clock and ending at 8 o'clock (Figure 0.1). Throughout our lifetime we have seen it in various places and presented in the assorted colors of the rainbow, whether it be big or small, handmade and commercially produced, worn by young and old, used by individuals and organizations. Perhaps we doodled it ourselves in a notebook or on a backpack. The peace symbol seems simple and innocuous enough, yes? Certainly not worthy of serious academic treatment to be distributed by a leading academic publication house. And definitely not by a psychologist. What could psychology meaningfully derive from and contribute to what many consider, at best, pop culture ephemera?

I used to ask myself that question too; then I became a depth psychologist.

For readers who may be unfamiliar with depth psychology, when Sigmund Freud broke with important predecessors in dynamic psychiatry, it was his approach, which would later be called *depth psychology*, that fueled "a cultural revolution comparable in scope to that unleashed by Darwin" (Ellenberger, 1970, p. 418). What sets depth psychology apart from other psychological approaches are its claims "to furnish a key to the exploration of the unconscious mind, and through this a renewed knowledge of the conscious mind, with wider application to the understanding of literature, art, religion, and culture" (p. 490). In this spirit, depth psychology takes seriously the work and efforts of the unconscious

DOI: 10.4324/b23325-1

Figure 0.1 ND/Peace Symbol. Credit: Matthew C. Clonch.

and pays close attention to how the unconscious may show itself through a culture's myths, symbols, folktales, dreams, art, cultural artifacts, theater, motion pictures, community murals, and so on and so forth. In addition to Freud, other pioneers in the field include analytical psychologists Carl G. Jung (1961, 1978, 1981, 2002) and Marie-Louise Von Franz (1980, 1993, 1995), individual and self-psychologists Alfred Adler (1927/1998) and Heinz Kohut (1985), object relations psychologists Melanie Klein (1975) and Donald Winnicott (1988), and archetypal psychologist James Hillman (1975, 1981, 2004).

When I searched for answers to the above questions, depth psychology offered an academic home and taxonomy to understand the world that was in line with my own persistent proclivities toward psychology, the humanities, and the interconnection between the two.

"As helpers from the West, what can we do from our position in the global north to aid Tibetans and Tibetans-in-exile in the struggle for liberation?" I inquired Dr. Tenzin Namdul many years ago while sitting in one of the well-worn classrooms of Men-Tsee-Khang, the Tibetan Medical and Astrological Institute of H.H. the Dalai Lama in Dharamsala, India. Looking out over the misty Himalayan mountainside, I distinctly remember Dr. Namdul's reply: "What Westerners can do to help us is to better understand our culture; to better understand our folk traditions and folk treatments; to better understand that we have a different definition, perspective, and meaning of time; and lastly, *you can help us by taking the time to understand how things work and not be so eager to fix*" (personal communication, April 30, 2002).

To this day, I distinctly remember that sunny early afternoon over 20 years ago, when Dr. Namdul's observation overturned my worldview. Not only did his response suggest that my desire to engage issues of social justice in the world did not restrict me to producing diagnoses, treatment plans, and to "fixing" people—as my formal psychology educational experiences had taught me—but that I could also be of service in the world by deeply listening to and understanding the interconnectedness between people, systems, institutions, power dynamics, cultures, and nature. Not only did the weight of this realization produce a paradigm shift for me, but it also released me from the etiologically bound medical model that dominates accepted Western standards of healing.

If you have experienced the power of a world-shifting idea before, you will understand when I share that I was suddenly and irrevocably engrossed by the possibilities presented by these new ontologies, epistemologies, and teleologies. The world was no longer as it had been before, and the momentum of this budding transformation, its flush and fire, sent me searching. I began researching liberation psychology and international peace work efforts grounded in the principles of liberation theory, feminism, Buddhist and depth psychology. Aiming to substantiate and enhance these paradigmatic inquiries, I travelled back and forth from Southeast Asia over the next 17 years to work with Thai peace and justice nongovernmental organizations, Thai women and women refugees from Burma, and groups of women activists from Sri Lanka, Cambodia, Bangladesh, Burma, India, and Thailand. Joining with Thai local partners and my U.S. psychologist mentor in the field, Dr. Kathryn Norsworthy, the National Human Rights Commission of Thailand sponsored our feminist and liberation psychology-based conflict resolution and peacebuilding workshops to work with ethnic-Malay Muslim and ethnic-Thai Buddhist community leaders involved in the ethnopolitically charged southern Thai border provinces.

The kindling for this ongoing and focused attention was a question that had been a companion of mine for many years, through many travels, and in many circumstances. The question was "What *is* peace…. really?" Holding this question as I moved about in local and global communities, my formally trained art history eye for symbols and visual representations honed in on how groups and organizations would (1) use *peace* as text to draw attention to, or to further, their cause, and (2) visually represent their cause in sign, brand, icon, emblem, or by means of other visual device. The range of causes and imagery under the banner of peace was astounding: from global issues such as old growth deforestation to local issues such as the endangered manatee population; from international relations in the Middle East to local relations with migrant farmworkers in the citrus or fern/houseplant industry; from higher education institutions designing cutting edge peace curricula to students signing up to receive advanced degrees in peace studies; from joining the federal government in organizations like the Peace Corps to supporting independent organizations like Greenpeace or Peace Jam; from military-contracted corporations making "bombs for peace," to those who call themselves peacemakers-peacebuilders-peaceworkers and protest for peace in the streets; from inter-intra spiritual peace practices to music, art, film, and community peace festivals. The list goes on and on.

Musing the hefty industry built upon notions of peace as well as the intentional channeling of affect around peace, I wondered whether we, as a collective, even knew what peace was. We were working so very tirelessly for peace—creating, calling, planning, networking, organizing, disseminating, campaigning, activating, producing, writing, performing, fundraising, selling—but, for what were we *really* doing it? Would we know what peace was if we were successful and "had it?" And, what I found to be most interesting is the following two-part question: How are we, as a cultural collective, registering this virtually unknown entity of *peace* into our visual cultural economy? How do visual representations or symbols of peace further social causes and which benefits can be gained from utilizing a peace symbol's cultural capital?

Firstly, there is a long and entrenched social, literary, artistic, cultural, and archival tradition of portraying *war* and *peace* as bifurcated, fixed, oppositional, and overdetermined. War tends to be prescribed as active, masculine, full, heteronormative, valorous, and as important to historical time. Conversely, peace tends to be prescribed as inactive, feminine, passive, simple, lacking, timid, and ahistorical. A byproduct of operating within this inherited cultural milieu is that the dominant ideologies shaping how *war* and *peace* ought to be understood also saturated my studies and research. In conversations with depth psychologists about *peace representations*, opinions fell into predictable categories. On one hand, people maintained that peace could not stand on its own as a topic because peace is simply the absence of war. "For one to 'rightly' investigate peace, one must investigate war," I was told. It was difficult to engage in conversations that diverged from the traditional masculine notions of peace as mere prologue or epilogue to war. On the other hand, peace was often understood as a function of war. That is, when I inquired about peace symbology or peace mythologies, I encountered enthusiastic and energetic discourses on militaristic strategies, Picasso's *Guernica*, and international relations. The advice was obvious: It is impossible to study peace outside of its fixed binary opposition to war, and that as a starting point, I must approach the topic through the binaries—first research *war*, then discuss *peace*.

One challenge to understanding and imagining *peace-as-effort* or *peace-as-energy-in-flux* is that these ideas are not readily evident in Western culture. As I have found in my experiences in the U.S. and abroad, it seems that we, particularly in the West, do not have wide or easy access to peace-centered language, mythologies, cultural stories, narratives, folktales, or images. It is from this perspective that an important depth psychological question arises. Does the relatively absent symbolic, mythological, and archetypal discourse on peace suggest that it has been culturally repressed, sublimated, or disinherited? Perhaps the constructive characteristics and possibilities of peace have been isolated from our culture's consciousness. And if this is the case, depth psychology would have us wonder whether this "shadow" might point toward a hidden collective and cultural "gold mine" of positive potentials, and would ask by which methods this obscured material might be unearthed.

Fortunately, there is a robust depth psychological tradition of investigating the interconnections between archetype, symbol, and mythology. These interconnections often reflect affect formation in the conscious/unconscious and cultural/collective, and depth psychology aims to understand how that affect is channeled or redirected back into the collective or individual with its subsequent actions or non-actions. Symbols such as the mandala, the grail, the cross, the circle, and flying saucers have received much attention in the extant body of depth psychological literature by scholars like C. G. Jung (1961, 1978, 1981), S. Freud (1900/1980, 1901/1981,

1930/1989), M. L. Von Franz (1980), and J. Jacobi (1959) among others. However, there seems to be little or no exploration into the symbolic and action-oriented realms of peace. In response to these lacunae, this book addresses an overlooked area in psychological studies of peace: the archetypal, symbolic, and mythological realms of peace and the ways in which social movements serve as conduits to propagate collective beliefs and ideas. To this end, the 1958 nuclear disarmament (ND) image (as the peace symbol was originally known) serves as our agent to investigate these depth psychological tenets.

The ND/peace symbol is an unconventional and complicated subject for case study research. In the 60+ years since its debut, the graphic is nearly ever-present all around the world and its mercurial nature encourages it to be endlessly transformed and transfigured by the contexts in which it emerges. Therefore, choosing an omnipresent artifact, or what Miles (2008) has called "world-wide shorthand for peace" (p. 224), mandates that strong and clear boundaries be placed, from the beginning, around what would be included *and* excluded from the inquiry. Although I have endeavored to deeply understand and capably describe how the peace symbol evolved and functioned in its associated liberation movements, a number of limitations merit attention.

One limitation is that the insights harvested on the ND/peace symbol have been analyzed from, and represent, a Western depth psychological perspective. Situating the work within a Western rubric of analysis is not intended to be, as Tarnas (2000) writes, a "triumphalist presumption that the West is somehow intrinsically superior to other civilizations and thus not worthy of our attention" (p. 252). Instead, the intention is to turn a critical eye toward the West's psychological landscape during a time when the bomb's early existence produced a new and strange power differential in global politics with the West harboring omnipotent nuclear weapons and choosing the Pacific as the site for continued atmospheric testing. If non-Western perspectives were included, different, yet crucially significant, results would most likely have been generated. Therefore, this book may seem limited in scope to those who deem that a more inclusive perspective would be better suited to interpret the emergence, fortitude, and atrophy of the peace symbol.

Introduction 7

A second area of note pertains to the criteria that were used to evaluate the peace symbol's functions in the liberation movements associated with it. For example, one criterion that I intentionally chose was to focus the inquiry primarily on the first seven years of the symbol's existence, from 1958 to 1965, with only a few exceptional data included from the years, 1965 to 1969. In this way, the case study focused primarily on the symbol's emergence and fortitude into the cultural visual canon in the West. Tracking the symbol's psycho-cultural-historical roots during these few short years, before its turn to ubiquity, roots out, for the most part, the gross misuses and misinterpretations of the symbol that abound from the mid-to-late 1960s to the present, and allows us to simply focus on its original psycho-social applications.

A few notes on the structure of this book: We cannot fully consider the peace symbol until we have understood the sociocultural-historical psyche that supplied the prenatal space for the peace symbol to eventually emerge, fortify, and propagate into the West's cultural consciousness. In other words, we have to dig deep to the root cause of why the symbol needed to be created in the first place. Other peace symbols such as the white dove and green olive branch were readily available for use and were already tacitly understood in the visual cultural economy, yet they were not chosen to represent the social movements of the day. Therefore, our investigation requires a launching point in the years preceding the U.S.'s mobilization into World War II (WWII), at a time after Orson Welles' 1938 *War of the Worlds* radio drama that produced invasion terror in the American psyche and before the atomic bomb, known colloquially as the Manhattan Project, was realized on the world stage through the invasive civilian bombings of Hiroshima and Nagasaki, Japan in 1945.

The book is divided into four analytical parts, each emphasizing different and germane depth psychological concepts. The order of presentation follows a historical chronology that builds upon itself to contextualize the psychological conditions present in the cultural milieu that contributed to the emergence of the ND image and the social movements for which it extensively labored.

Part I—Shadow: A shifting and developing concept, as is common for most theories concerning the unconscious, the shadow is a dynamic challenge for its researchers. In *The Archetypes and the Collective Unconscious* (1981), Jung states that the shadow "personifies everything that the subject refuses to acknowledge about himself and yet is always thrusting itself upon him directly or indirectly—for instance, inferior traits of character and other incompatible tendencies" (pp. 284–285). I lean into Jung's theoretical concept of the shadow and we'll go more in depth into shadow at the individual and collective levels focusing on the U.S. government's Manhattan Engineer District's (MED) development during the years between 1939 and 1945.

Part II–Enantiodromia: In its most basic understanding across cultures, time and philosophical traditions, enantiodromia is the reversal of one extreme into its opposite. Jung negatively correlates his perspective on enantiodromia with his concept of the psychological shadow. He notes that "as in its collective, mythological form, so also the individual shadow contains within it the seed of enantiodromia, of a conversion into its opposite" (Van Eenwyk, 1997, p. 93). Part II investigates enantiodromian processes from 1945 to 1958 as the Western psyche grapples with the knowledge and evidence that humans can now globally self-annihilate—which was once placed solely in the gods and goddesses' loci of control. We will look at a series of cultural artifacts, cinematic movies, and other means of collective devices used to understand the newly materialized atomic age and world order. These processes set the conditions for the endemic ND image, later known as the peace symbol, to materialize and be an effective herald of the age's emotions of despair and courage.

Part III–Symbol: Whereas symbols have a rich history in art, religion, literature, and culture, they also have profuse roots in psychology, and particularly in depth psychology. In essence, symbols can be understood as an interface of human consciousness to the unconscious, at both individual and collective levels. Archetypal symbols emerge out of a collective and repeated response to an idea, quality, or condition that finds form and visual representation in a recursive glyph. In 1958—13 years after the atomic bombs detonated on Japan's civilian populace—the psycho-emotional matrix that the collective found itself in, with three nation states possessing nuclear weapons and with France within two years of procuring its nuclear weapons program, provided the interface and the archetypal predilection toward survival, to beget what we now know as the peace symbol.

Part IV–Kairos: The crucial moment when conditions are just so, that action or movement forward is possible and all but avoidable, is the essence of kairos. Kairos neither concerns itself with seconds, hours, days, weeks, months, or years. Nor does it employ watches, clocks, or calendars. Similar to mother nature's approach to time; where dandelions do not bloom at a particular time and date on the Julian calendar (chronos), but only when all the conditions are just so—the sunlight, the soil and its nutrients, the water, the climate's temperature, the depth of the seed—does the daffodil root and bloom. In these cases, kairos, not chronos, is in charge of setting the time for action. Part IV more closely considers kairos as we investigate the social movements that arose and utilized the peace symbol in their efforts toward peace and justice.

While the shadow receives the bulk of depth psychology's examination, William Miller (1989) embraces the oft-bypassed positive possibilities of the shadow and calls it the golden shadow in *Your Golden Shadow: Discovering and Fulfilling Your Undeveloped Self*. According to Miller, the persona and shadow have enantiodromian qualities: "for every trait, characteristic, attitude, and aptitude that we draw up into the persona, its opposite—equal in magnitude—we reject and relegate to the shadow side" (p. 10). Miller champions an inversion of the traditional shadow notion by suggesting that we also possess a golden shadow made up of positive traits that were not valued by family, subculture, community, or culture. Part IV investigates the golden shadow concept in relation to kairos and how these two concepts work together to produce an unparalleled era of activism and social action in the late 1950s and into the 1960s.

In the 65 years since the peace symbol's nativity, we have witnessed this singular and ubiquitous modern symbol assume prime real estate on protest placards and be employed to lead marches, we have seen it scribbled and graffitied on subways and on the sides of buildings all around the globe, we wear it on T-shirts, buttons, socks, jewelry, and handbags, and we have seen it embed itself into pop culture through movie posters—most notably Stanley Kubrick's *Full Metal Jacket* (1987)—and in TV shows such as *Fortunate Son* (2020). For those of us in the U.S., it defines the 1960s, an era of flower power, peace, and protest against the Vietnam War. At once ubiquitously present in pop culture and yet with an unknown origin story, the peace symbol has a unique history in the pantheon of peace symbols utilized in the West's modern era.

References

Adler, A. (1998). *Understanding human nature* (C. Brett, Trans). Center City, MN: Hazeldon. (Original work published 1927)
Dennis, J. (2020). Fortunate Son. Lark Productions.
Ellenberger, H. F. (1970). *Discovery of the unconscious: The history and evolution of dynamic psychiatry*. New York, NY: Basic Books.
Freud, S. (1980). *On dreams* (J. Strachey, Trans.). New York, NY: W. W. Norton. Original work published 1900)
Freud, S. (1981). *The psychopathology of everyday life* (J. Strachey, Trans.). New York, NY: W. W. Norton. (Original work published 1901)
Freud, S. (1989). *Civilization and its discontents* (J. Strachey, Trans.). New York, NY: W. W. Norton. (Original work published 1930)
Hillman, J. (1975). *Revisioning psychology*. New York, NY: Harper and Row.
Hillman, J. (1981). Silver and the white earth (part two). *Spring: An Annual of Archetypal Psychology and Jungian Thought*, 21–66. Dallas, TX: Spring.
Hillman, J. (2004). *A terrible love of war*. New York, NY: The Penguin Press.
Jacobi, J. (1959). *Complex, archetype, symbol in the psychology of C. G. Jung*. New York, NY: Bollingen.
Jung, C. G. (1961). *Memories, dreams, reflections*. New York, NY: Vintage Books.
Jung, C. G. (1978). *Flying saucers: A modern myth of things seen in the skies*. New York, NY: MJF Books.
Jung, C. G. (1981). *Archetypes and the collective unconscious*. Princeton, NJ: Princeton University Press.
Jung, C. G. (2002). Nature was once fully spirit *and* matter. In M. Sabini (Ed.), *The Earth has a soul: Nature writings of C. G. Jung* (pp. 79–88). Berkeley, CA: North Atlantic Books.
Klein, M. (1975). *Love, guilt and reparation and other works 1921–1945*. New York, NY: The Free Press.
Kohut, H. (1985). *Self psychology and the humanities: Reflections on a new psychoanalytic approach*. New York, NY: W. W. Norton.
Kubrick, S. (1987). *Full Metal Jacket*. Warner Bros.
Miles, B. (2008). *Peace: 50 years of protest*. Pleasantville, NY: Reader's Digest Association.
Miller, W. A. (1989). *Your golden shadow: Discovering and fulfilling your undeveloped self*. San Francisco, CA: Harper & Row.

Tarnas, R. (2000). Is the modern psyche undergoing a rite of passage? In T. Singer (Ed.), *The vision thing: Myth, politics and psyche in the world* (pp. 251–267). New York, NY: Routledge.
Van Eenwyk, J. R. (1997). *Archetypes and strange attractors: The chaotic world of symbols.* Toronto: Inner City Books.
Von Franz, M-L. (1980). *Alchemy: An introduction to the symbolism and the psychology.* Toronto: Inner City Books.
Von Franz, M-L. (1993). *The feminine in fairy tales.* Boston, MA: Shambhala.
Von Franz, M-L. (1995). *Shadow and evil in fairytales.* Boston, MA: Shambhala.
Welles, O. (1938, October). War of the Worlds: Mercury Theater original radio broadcast. Retrieved from www.loc.gov/static/programs/natio nal-recording-preservation-board/documents/TheWaroftheWorlds.pdf
Winnicott, D. W. (1988). *Human nature.* New York, NY: Brunner/Mazel.

Part I: Shadow
Cultural Secret Detonated

As promised, our case study of the ND image/peace symbol starts in the years preceding the U.S.'s mobilization into WWII, when numerous countries were working fastidiously and furtively to create military advantages on the war front. In the shadows of the West's public consciousness, a hulking secret was being created, developed, and formalized that, once revealed, immediately changed the course of human history. It is here, in these dire and precarious times, we initiate our inquiry into the historical and psychological conditions that ultimately fashion and forge the peace symbol into the pantheon of modern peace symbols.

Psychological Shadow

Calling upon classic German literature to help elucidate the shadow notion in his autobiography *Memories, Dreams, Reflections* (1961), Swiss psychologist Carl Jung, former protégé of Sigmund Freud, recalls a time from his youth when he was "caught up" (p. 235) by Goethe's story of Faust encountering the "dark side of his being, his sinister shadow" (p. 235) in Mephistopheles. We learn from depth psychology that literature is an effective and efficient device to illustrate psychological concepts, and in the case of the shadow, characters like Wilde's Dorian Gray (1998), Stevenson's Dr. Jekyll and Mr. Hyde (2008), Poe's narrator in *The Tell-Tale Heart* (1983), Shakespeare's Iago from *Othello* (1993), DC comics' "Two-Face" in the Batman series (Gaiman, Grant, & Verheiden, 1989), Elphaba and Glenda from G. Maguire's (1995) *Wicked: The Life and Times of the Wicked Witch of the West*, and J. K. Rowling's

(2004) Delores Umbridge from the Harry Potter series instruct us well.

Recall from the Introduction that in *The Archetypes and the Collective Unconscious* (1981), Jung states that the shadow "personifies everything that the subject refuses to acknowledge about himself and yet is always thrusting itself upon him directly or indirectly—for instance, inferior traits of character and other incompatible tendencies" (pp. 284–285). As his career and theories matured, Jung consistently refined and redefined his understanding of the shadow, allowing for more fluidity and expansion in his stance rather than rigidity and contraction. For example, in *Aion* (1959), he offers a rich and more encompassing perspective of the shadow:

> The shadow [is] that hidden, repressed, for the most part inferior and guilt-laden personality whose ultimate ramifications reach back into the realm of our animal ancestors and so compromise the whole historical aspect of the unconscious... .If it has been believed hitherto that the human shadow was the source of all evil, it can now be ascertained on closer investigation that the unconscious man, that is, his shadow, does not consist only of morally reprehensible tendencies, but also displays a number of good qualities, such as normal instincts, appropriate reactions, realistic insights, creative impulses, etc.
>
> (p. 266)

The last two lines of this passage deserve additional attention as it relates to our topic, and we will do just so in Part IV. For now, however, let's keep the attention on the customary understanding of shadow and notice how the post-Jungians also endeavor to comprehend the nuances of the shadow concept.

Samuels, Shorter, and Plaut (1986), in a popular and base characterization of the *shadow*, contend that it contains the parts of our personality that we wish to hide and conceal. It is our inferior and threatening side, the sum of all of our unpleasant qualities. The *shadow* is coupled with the center of consciousness, the *ego*—also known as the persona, or the "accessible" interface between the individual and the society. Whichever personality characteristics the ego deems useful will become part of the ego artifice. Whichever personality characteristics the ego deems not useful, or harmful to its societal survival, will be relegated to the shadow. Stevens (1999) extends this definition, adding that the shadow "has [as] its archetypal core—the archetype of the enemy, the treacherous stranger, the evil intruder" (p. 45). Likewise, Stein (1998) posits that most people "only reveal shadowy elements by accident, in dreams, or when pushed to extremes" (p. 108). Storr (1983) alludes to a more encompassing understanding and multivalent qualities in his glossary entry, *shadow*:

> The inferior part of the personality; sum of all personal and collective psychic elements which, because of their incompatibility with the chosen conscious attitude, are denied expression in life and therefore coalesce into a relatively autonomous "splinter personality" with contrary tendencies in the unconscious. The shadow behaves compensatorily to consciousness; hence its effects can be positive as well as negative.
>
> (p. 422)

Lastly, Hopcke (1999) understands Jung to suggest that we may also "project the shadow onto others, attributing to other people those nasty, unsavory qualities that we would like to deny in ourselves. Shadow projection can thus result in paranoia, suspiciousness.... all of which afflict individuals, groups, even entire nations" (p. 84).

As concepts primarily utilized for individuals in analysis, there have also been numerous scholars, in addition to Hopcke (1999), who have extrapolated the notions of the *shadow* and *ego* to the cultural and collective level (Hillman, 2004; Jung, 1978; Samuels, 1993; Singer, 2000; Singer & Kimbles, 2004; Zweig & Abrams, 1991). Following their lead, a shadow analysis is applied to the cultural and collective and into the nuclear disarmament (ND) image as a post-WWII (and post-atomic bomb) response.

Now we will swivel our attention toward the institutionalized and systematic use of secrecy to uphold the government's parameters and knowledges in its military, industrial, and civilian sectors during WWII, and toward the severe efforts its stewards took to ensure that information did not leak out into the country's collective consciousness.

Cultural Secret: The Manhattan Project

In the years preceding the war, an understood and ethical practice of the international scientific community was to share and widely distribute one's research and discoveries. Free exchange of information was necessary for ideas and theories to cross-pollinate, build upon each other, and create new possibilities. This was particularly the case prior to 1939, when scientists tended to work in academic institutions, rely on published reports or personal correspondences with colleagues for information, and work within the limits of department-determined budget lines (Kelly, 2007; Schweber, 2000). The civilian scientific community was not often called upon to engage in matters of public policy, military warfare, or international politics. With the onset of WWII, however, and the concurrent revolutionary discoveries in nuclear energy and nuclear weapons technologies, the necessity to protect proprietary information and supremely advanced warfare technologies steadily incapacitated the scientific community's ethos of timely information exchange (Giegerich, 2007; Kelly, 2007; Schweber, 2000).

Without a background check, government clearance, and involvement in government funded research, not only would a scientist be restricted from the research advancements made in nuclear fission, but her or his chances of securing funds for high-tech research instruments would also be diminished. "Gone were the days when an experimental physicist could do important and imaginative work by himself without adequate support to construct the necessary equipment and to purchase many of the [required] instruments" (Schweber, 2000, p. 9). Further compounding this scientific knowledge access issue is the 20th-century physicist's dependence on "large and expensive pieces of equipment—cyclotrons, betatrons, Van der Graaf generators, cryostats, nuclear reactors—to carry out their research, equipment that the government was willing to underwrite lavishly" (p. 9). By the early years of WWII, nuclear physicists' ethical double bind was becoming self-evident: If physicists wanted to continue working on eminent developments and technologies in the thermo-nuclear field *and* receive appropriate funding for specialized and necessary equipment, they would be required to hedge the ethos of their civilian profession and work for the military, work for the war effort, and bequeath all information or discovery to the government. If they morally and ethically objected to laboring for the war effort, or were staunchly invested in the civilian science principle of free and timely information exchange, their access would be restricted from the leading edges of theoretical or applied thermonuclear knowledge production.

One month before Nazi Germany invaded Poland in September 1939, the benchmark event many historians consider to have launched WWII, U.S. President Franklin D. Roosevelt received an urgent hand-delivered letter from physicist and German émigré, Albert Einstein, regarding the possible development of a nuclear weapons program by Germany (Kelly, 2007). Einstein urged the president to look immediately into nuclear energy research as a matter of U.S. national security (Kelly, 2007). He noted that new and dazzling discoveries in thermonuclear physics—the nuclear chain reaction in particular—made it possible for countries with access to resources to create a nuclear weapons program with "extremely powerful bombs" (p. 43) capable of inconceivable destruction. To quicken any governmental biding, Einstein disclosed that according to his resources, Germany had already taken the atypical step of stopping the sale of uranium from their recently acquired uranium mines in former Czechoslovakia (Kelly, 2007). Enriched quantities of the element uranium are necessary for the production of nuclear bombs, and such a seemingly calculated and early step on the part of Germany was understood by American physicists to indicate Germany's avid desire to repeat the experiments and work already done by U.S. physicists (Kelly, 2007; Dahl, 1999). Einstein warned that the U.S. needed to exercise "watchfulness" and that "quick action" (Kelly, 2007, p. 43) would be necessary from the administration in what, in his estimation, was surely to become the nuclear arms race (Giegerich, 2007; Schweber, 2000; Dahl, 1999).

Two months later, in October 1939, and one month after Germany's invasion of Poland, Einstein received a curt written reply from President Roosevelt thanking him for his "most interesting and important enclosure" (Kelly, 2007, p. 44), and reciprocally disclosing that he "found the data of such import that I have convened a Board consisting of the head of the Bureau of Standards" (p. 44), along with a few elite military officials to "thoroughly investigate the possibility of your suggestion regarding the element of uranium" (p. 44). Although it was not officially named at this moment in time, the Manhattan Project had commenced at President Roosevelt's orders, and it would not be until three years later in 1942 that the project would receive its official nomenclature under the supervision of the Army Corps of Engineers: the Manhattan Engineer District, the "MED," or more simply known by the moniker "The Manhattan Project" (Kelly, 2007; Giegerich, 2007; Schweber, 2000; Dahl, 1999). Between the six years of 1939 and 1945, the top secret U.S.-based Manhattan Project involved three countries (U.S., Britain, and production sites in Canada); research, production, procurement, and manufacturing sites in 17 of the 48 contiguous states; academic institutions such as Harvard, Princeton, and Columbia universities, MIT, the University of Chicago, and UC-Berkeley, to name but a few; federal employment of approximately 130,000 people; and cost nearly $2 billion dollars ($32.5 billion by today's inflation calculations [US Inflation Calculator n.d.]) (Kelly, 2007; Giegerich, 2007; Schweber, 2000).

Today, we have access to numerous books, research, and memorial museums that well document the moral, nationalistic, and logical reasons why individuals agreed, or did not agree, to be involved with the Manhattan Project (Giegerich, 2007; Kelly, 2007; Rotblat & Ikeda, 2007; Schweber, 2000; Bird & Lifschultz, 1998). With virtually full compliance, unless they possessed highly specialized or exceptional skills, MED employees did not know the true telos of their work and labor. During a time when Rosie the Riveter's "We Can Do It!" spoke to both female and male civilian workers of the war effort, MED employees believed that they were helping America win the war, but they were informed of no more than was necessary to complete the immediate task of their assignment (Kelly, 2007). For instance, the manufacturing employees who were tasked with creating nuts and bolts did not know for which military endeavors their nuts and bolts would be used (for any number of nuclear instruments, machines, nuclear reactors, or storage warehouses). Or, for the employees in the laboratory who were charged with maintaining temperatures and atmospheric pressure, they did not know for what, precisely, they were maintaining temperatures or atmospheric pressure, but they knew their job was to uphold orders from unit superiors and to report any anomalies that occurred during their shift (Kelly, 2007). For the majority of the 130,000 employees of the MED, their experience was akin to being a solitary cog in the machine, an isolated spoke on the wheel, or an ad-hoc rendering of the homogenizing assembly line practice of Fordism.

Mythology Aplenty: Archetypal Frontier, Apocalypse, Modern-Day Alchemy and Pygmalion

In its most basic essence, an archetype is a pattern of behavior and/or attributes of humans, animals or places that transcend local contexts and are global in nature. For example, for the Queen archetype, it does not matter where in the world the Queen lives, we have a sense of her role (pattern of behavior and attributes) in her society. If the archetype is of the Teacher, again, it does not matter which content the teacher is teaching or where they are located, we have a sense of their role in the community. We can say this about a number of different archetypal roles that inhabit our consciousness—court jester or class clown, villain, priest, crone, apprentice, healer, teacher's pet, and the list goes on. Dogs are often known to be loyal, lions to be courageous, temples to be sacred and transcendent, and watering holes/bars to be the place of chance meetings between a wide assortment of characters. In fact, it is archetypal characters and settings which bring mythologies, folk tales, fairy tales, movies, books, and community murals to life.

Jung further developed the archetype concept through a psychological lens asserting that archetypes are bipolar in that they have both positive and negative sides, more specifically "a positive, favorable bright side that point upward [and a] partly negative and unfavorable, partly chthonic side" (as quoted in Van Eenwyk, 1997, p. 91). We can imagine the Queen archetype as having both light and dark potentialities in her wholeness. In her positive light side of the archetype, she is benevolent, caring, a role model, and majestic. In her negative dark side, she may be icy cold, calculating, and ruthless. Jung argues that archetypes cannot be "adequately expressed by anything actual, just as a whole cannot be adequately defined by one of its parts" (1959, p. 23). Thus, as we endeavor to understand both the "parts" and the "whole" of the peace symbol's existence, we will look specifically at how the ego and the shadow, positive and negative components of the Self archetype (Jung, 1959) respectively, interacted consciously through different registers and scales of the MED, and continued on through to the emergence of Britain's Campaign for Nuclear Disarmament (CND) and the subsequent Peace movement in the U.S.

To help us understand the centrality of archetype and myth that fueled the psychic energy of the Manhattan Project, psychologist James Hillman's cultural observations from *A Terrible Love of War* (2004) suggest that despite the ubiquity and constancy of war throughout recorded history, fundamental shifts occur at each epoch reliant and dependent upon the technologies *and* imagination available to a particular nation-state or rogue group in any given moment. For Hillman, the modern-day battlefield experiences

> different styles of war under the aegis of different gods with different styles of imagination. Instead of Mars/Ares, the strategies and political indoctrination of Athene, wars of words and leaflets, winning the hearts and minds, conversion to reason, and the long-term planning of countermeasures to the long-term planning of hijackers and plotters. Instead of Mars, Hermes… . undercover infiltration, code-breaking, jamming, surveillance. … . Yet, more threatening is the imagination of Apollo, "the fardarter," as he was called, who killed with arrows shot through the air: the imagination of distancing. Weapons far from the front, the front itself dissolved as war moves upward into the air, to satellites, outer space, transformed by the Appollonic imagination into nuclear visions brighter than a thousand suns.
>
> (pp. 90–91)

Indeed, the nuclear age presents myriad unfamiliar and distinct considerations, ramifications, and consequences on which to pore over. Hillman laments that post-WWII warfare is "with no foreseeable end in time or limit in target, equal in concept to the totalizing power of its instruments, and is monotheistic in essence" (p. 21). Perhaps there is truth in his ideas and the question remains: In the 75+ years since we first actualized the bomb, has it successfully plodded its way to the status of an omnipotent (demi)god?

By 1940, the U.S. mainland had been organized into 48 states and it was 19 years before the 49th state, Alaska, would join the union. With the continental Manifest Destiny achieved—the government agenda of conquering Native American land in North America, from the Atlantic seaboard to the Pacific Ocean, or "sea to shining sea"—and an insidious and rhizomatic cultural Manifest Destiny persisting, the institutionalized and structural urge for conquering and taming exotic new lands, peoples, and species (i.e., colonialism) prompted a yearning for a *new* frontier, or a *new* wild west, and found an eventual homestead in the vast frontier of nuclear science technology (and, about 13 years after the Manhattan Project, aeronautics and space technology would become the new Manifest Destiny frontier [Romanyshyn, 1989]). Nuclear and quantum physics were amateur fields at the time and initial research and experiments nearly guaranteed a wellspring of possibilities, discoveries, and advancements just beyond their existing precipices (Dahl, 1999; Brodie, 1946; Wendt & Geddes, 1945).

Generally speaking, the allure of the archetypal frontier is its promise of *getting away from* the drab or colorless place one currently dwells and *moving toward* a fresh, untread upon, and fantasized paradise offering full bounty (May, 1991). For the U.S., as it distanced itself *away from* Mother Europe and with its steady centuries-in-the-making progress *toward* individuated world power status, "the frontier was.... the crucial myth; [and] its special characteristics became distinctly American" (p. 93). With the ominous threat of U.S. involvement in WWII—the U.S. did not officially enter the war until after the bombings of Pearl Harbor in December 1941—and equipped with credible intelligence that Germany was most likely concurrently pursuing a nuclear weapons program (Kelly, 2007; Schweber, 2000), the U.S. easily shunted the pooled affect and urges around the unemployed and somewhat defunct "frontiersman" image into the image of a promised land of nuclear weapons technologies. For the MED, nuclear physicist J. Robert Oppenheimer and Army General Leslie R. Groves became a 20th-century Lewis and Clark expedition team chartered by their president to explore unknown and unmapped territories, only to return and bequeath any prized acquisitions to the U.S. government.

What was the MED's draw for the ordinary civilian physicist? With closer attention to the mythical underpinnings of the cultural landscape, we see that some aspects of the Manhattan Project's mythos have their roots in the American frontier and explorer archetype, whereas other aspects seem to be rooted in the Biblical myth of the Apocalypse. Edward Edinger (1999) offers a useful etymological understanding of the word *apocalypse* in *Archetype of the Apocalypse* and it offers an entry point for our inquiry. He notes:

> *Apokalypsis* is just the Greek word that was used for the Book of Revelation which is also more simply called the Apocalypse; in general the term means "revelation." But, specifically, it refers to the "uncovering of what has been hidden." The root is the verb *kalypto,* which means "to cover or to hide"; the prefix is the preposition, *apo,* which means "away or from." So, *apokalypsis* means "to take the covering away" from what had been secret or covered—revealing thereby what had previously been invisible. Yet according to general usage, the term "apocalypse" has taken on the larger meaning of the "coming of deity to assert sovereignty "—or the coming of a Messiah to judge, to reward or punish humanity.
>
> (pp. 2–3)

It is easy to understand, how, in retrospect, "general usage" apocalyptic fears emerged in 1940s America among a collective worried that the end of humankind was near. In the span of less than a quarter century the populace endured the loss of loved ones in WWI, they experienced the mass panic and hysteria of Orson Welles' *War of the Worlds*—a "live" radio narrative of a supposed alien invasion with an alien-led heralding of the mythic final battle of Armageddon (Welles, 1938), and they witnessed the beginnings of WWII.

However, if we continue Edinger's line of etymological reasoning, it is possible that the generally accepted apocalypse myth—complete with four horsemen—might have had a different, yet vital, subtext for the MED physicist; a subtext in alignment with its etymological roots. At the very core of their work, nuclear physicists were first charged with the task of detecting the previously hidden subatomic universe, and second, to deeply understand and render the invisible cosmos *visible* to an ardent scientific community. Once the subatomic cover was taken away, the nuclear physicists' reformulated charge became analogous to the telos of alchemical metallurgy—essentially to try to create (nuclear) gold from lead. One can imagine the physicists resembling medieval alchemists . . . being responsible for treating the element of uranium after others removed it from the womb of the "leaden" earth; carefully handling the uranium while heating it up in a hermetic cauldron or vessel, now called a nuclear reactor; tending to the metamorphous substances; and harnessing the results in their most prized forms. For the nuclear physicist, the philosopher's stone—the alchemist's gold transmuted from lead—was a bomb with a flash of light brighter than gold. Indeed, the new philosopher's stone was a power-*full* bomb with, to reference a post-nuclear bomb cliché from 1951's Federal Civil Defense Administration film *Duck and Cover* (Archer Productions), "a light brighter than the sun."

Wolfgang Giegerich, in *Technology and the Soul: From the Nuclear Bomb to the World Wide Web* (2007), articulates what, in his opinion, is the familiar interconnection between the nuclear-bomb-as-symbol, fairy tale, and archetype. He puts forward a fairy tale from the Brothers Grimm about the bottle imp, or the Spirit in the Glass, and overlays onto it the archetypal image of the Bomb. Mercurius, "a highly dangerous substance personified as a demon" (p. 102), is encapsulated in a sealed bottle. Anyone who cannot resist Mercurius' call from within the bottle, "let me out, let me out," can simply crack the seal that keeps the "explosive in a bottle" (p. 102). Once Mercurius is let out, "the spirit of the substance, which as long as it was contained in the bottle seemed small and harmless… . will explode out of the bottle and take on tremendous proportions, threatening to kill its liberator" (p. 102). Giegerich's connection between this cultural story, archetype, and symbol rings true. There *is* a familiarity with the archetypal events of this particular fairy tale; we have read about it in Mary Shelley's *Frankenstein* (2011), we have viewed the modern-day Pygmalion in Eliza Doolittle's character in *My Fair Lady* (Shaw & Lerner, 2006); and we have witnessed children play in the sandbox with a Godzilla figurine. Godzilla, of course, is the mythologically dormant ocean creature that absorbs radioactive byproducts in Tokyo Bay and reawakens from a 1,000-year hibernation to cause indiscriminate mass destruction in Japan (Tanaka & Honda,1954).

The bottle imp, the demon Mercurius—the spirit of the substance, which as long as it was contained in the bottle seemed an innocuous half-pint (Van Eenwyk, 1997), also works as a metaphor for the depth psychological notion of ego, the center of consciousness, or our public-facing persona. The metaphor's emphasis on the need for a façade (however thick or thin, it offers some amount of protection to its inside contents), and for there to be something with which the external can interact beyond the material glass, veneer, or psychological mask is useful for our analysis. The ego, like Mercurius, is reasonable when it is easily and consciously living within its socially prescribed perimeters, and like Mercurius still, the ego also embodies shadow aspects or potentials simply waiting for the appropriate opportunity or provocation to emerge from its sealed off quarters.

From the two images of the nuclear-physicist-as-a-modern-day-alchemist and the bottle imp, we can again imagine the MED nuclear physicists hunched over tables, tempted by the mercurial nature of the nuclear problematic, responding to the call of danger—the danger if she or he responds, the danger if she or he does not respond. Which individual will "liberate," to use Giegerich's term, the secret to the thermonuclear universe and craft one of the greatest scientific discoveries of the 20th century? Which scientific community will triumph in the nuclear arms race, "take home the gold," and be credited for saving their country from the demonized Other? It is hard to imagine dwelling in such an omnipotent, titillating, and frightening psychological nexus for a period of years.

Ego and Shadow Tarry Together

Reentering the timeline are the modern-day Lewis and Clark team, J. Robert Oppenheimer and Army General Groves. While Oppenheimer was charged with the confidential scientific responsibilities of the Manhattan Project, General Groves was charged with the project's clandestine logistics and pragmatics. With carte blanche power and funding from President Roosevelt and congressional leaders, Groves oversaw the *entire* project himself (Kelly, 2007). He selected the three "principal secret cities" of Los Alamos, NM; Oak Ridge, TN; and Hanford, WA for their isolated geographical sites—incredulously guaranteeing that "they were not on any maps during WWII" (Kelly, 2007, p. 155); conceived the industrial complexes that housed the various parts of the project as well as the segregated living quarters for 125,000 employees in its secret off the grid cities; designed security measures for covert activities happening in numerous cities in the U.S. and abroad; and also operated the program "on a need-to-know basis by the use of compartmentalization" (Kelly, 2007, p. 234). As the classified operation's architect, General Groves designed a network of disconnected and tactical operations to ensure that he was the "only person knowledgeable about the entire project" and the only one who could put *all* the pieces of the Manhattan Project puzzle together. Intending to thwart high-level espionage efforts, he single-handedly engineered and operationalized the most intense, vast, and centralized secret security supersystem up to that point in recorded Western history (Kelly, 2007; Schweber, 2000).

Thus, as a key central figure, General Groves gives us a glimpse into just how integral the individual ego/shadow scale is to the MED. As it developed in scope and size, so did General Groves' responsibilities; he operated as an omniscient personification of the Manhattan Project, the center of its consciousness, as well as its omnipotent actor. He hid, he covered over, he secreted, he divided, and he prevailed: He acted as a one-person decision tree determining when measures or actions would be taken, whether they would be implemented as individual or collective actions, and whether the actions would be typical or unique. Although his superiors saw him as sharp, trustworthy, and capable of leading the MED (the project *did* succeed with rapid results), Colonel Kenneth Nichols (2007), who oversaw the construction and operation of all MED facilities, described his supervisor as

> the biggest S.O.B I have ever worked for. He is most demanding. He is most critical. He is always a driver, never a praiser. He is abrasive and sarcastic. He disregards all normal organizational channels. He is extremely intelligent. He has the guts to make timely, difficult decisions. He is the most egotistical man I know. He knows he is right and so sticks by his decision. He abounds with energy and expects everyone to work as hard, or even harder, than he does... . . If I had to do my part of the atomic bomb project over again and had the privilege of picking my boss, I would pick General Groves.
>
> (p. 121)

Colonel Nichols' observations are an example par excellence of the interdependent notions of the ego and the shadow (notice his choice word, *egotistical*, and how it hovers between a spectrum of constructive character traits—ego—and arrogant/pompous traits—shadow). Whereas General Groves' expression of the ego archetype is as an intelligent hard worker who is able to be counted upon when tough decisions need to be made quickly, his expression of the shadow archetype is as a critical, demanding, and arrogant aggressor who can be counted upon to deliver abrasive and sarcastic reprobation. In this case, it is not a large leap to understand General Groves as a peculiar manifestation of the archetypal Dr. Jekyll and Mr. Hyde character; able to draw upon socially acceptable and adaptable traits when necessary, and allowing less acceptable traits to "escape" when in less rigidly structured environments (e.g., when he is in a superior position and not needing to save face with his own superiors).

The personal shadow can therefore be understood as a composite of external observations, internal perceptions, external encounters, and internal experiences that we do not consider to be us—we learn at some point in our maturation process that they are not acceptable to our subcultures, nor will they be rewarded, and we respond by elbowing these lived experiences back into the personal un/subconscious (Miller, 1989). When this same composite happens at the level of groups of people or cultures, the collective shadow is activated. Miller (1989) describes this process as the "more monolithic, rigid, demanding, authoritarian, narrow, and legalistic the immediate environment in which one develops [the military, or the MED for example], the thicker is the persona and the more massive is the shadow" (p. 13). In this spirit, the MED can also be understood as a stand-alone entity developing its own psychological schemas of ego and shadow. Just as we see in the individual of General Groves, where the ego and shadow tarry together and are ready to be of service when an opportunity presents, the MED too has a cultural level ego and shadow that tarry together. According to Jung (1959), the ego and shadow archetypes have significant parts to "play in the psychic economy" (p. 6).

Although the sheer magnitude of support the MED received from the U.S. Administration and its military branches is not remarkable in and of itself, it is the impenetrable and unparalleled cloak of secrecy, even amongst the top tier of government officials, which is singularly and historically remarkable. At the base of these extreme secrecy measures was the fear of possible Axis Powers espionage in the military, industrial, and civilian employee sectors of the Manhattan Project—a fear that, if accurate, would theoretically give the Axis Powers the military advantage in deciding the outcome of WWII (Giegerich, 2007; Kelly, 2007; Schweber, 2000; Bird & Lifschultz, 1998). The possibility that Germany not only was likely to have a jumpstart on nuclear weapon technologies (vis-à-vis Einstein's "canary in the mine" letter to FDR), but that they had easy access to mass quantities of *quality* uranium ores, urged the U.S. government to believe that any and all information relating to the development of U.S. nuclear weapons technologies must be enveloped in unprecedented security measures; if only for the fact that they did not want their knowledges, technologies, and products *to be used against them.*

In *A Terrible Love of War* (2004), Hillman writes, "the mind of war abstracts itself into signs and symbols, acronyms and units" (p. 46). Such was the case in the MED, and one way for us to make sense of the MED's compulsive need—the military's need—to code in signs and symbols, acronyms, and units is to understand that it served and labored for the benefit of the MED's shadow. Hillman amplifies this notion by stressing that a utilitarian ontology, as found in military strategy rooms, allows its colluders to "reduce qualities to numbers—measurement, calculation, computation, simply 'counting off,' and dog tags with blood type and serial number" (p. 52). He further states "the ontology of numerical thinking, of science itself,…. produces the impersonalization which creates a new kind of deliberate cruelty in the precisely calculated bombing of the unnamed by the unnamed" (p. 52).

Cultural Secret Detonated

So, it is the multilayered web of secrecy; the institutionally encouraged psychological and physical disassociation from the front-line battlefield; the will of the individual do-gooder ego and its desire to be acknowledged and rewarded; the thrill of adventure, loyalty, and camaraderie in a special operations unit; conquering a new world and "planting mother country's flag in its fruitful soil"; the fear of being ensnared on the erroneous side of the apocalyptic future; the ability of modern warfare to numericalize its technologies; and the government's willingness indiscriminately and prolifically to support the MED's leadership that led to the development of its complex and deep shadow potentials. Still, much individual and nationalist pride was at stake, and even with strictly designed security measures in place, secrets in general, "have a way of trying to emerge. Every secret is propelled by hidden inner forces toward human consciousness, and for this reason evil deeds eventually emerge into the awareness of humanity in general, or in someone in particular" (Sanford, 1991, p. 33). As the MED rocketed toward completion and toward General Groves' covert aim to "achieve military surprise when the bomb was used and thus gain the psychological effect" (Norris, 2007, p. 234), scientists began breaking their silence, speaking their consciousness with each other, and writing manifestos and reports advising against the military use of the bomb. Two such reports were *The Franck Report* of June 11, 1945 (Federation of American Scientists, n.d.) and *A Petition to the President of the United States* of July 17, 1945 from the Metallurgical Laboratory and Oak Ridge, TN Manhattan Project scientists (Kelly, 2007, pp. 292–293).

For the everyday citizen of the early 1940s, life-changing technological advances were marketed, experienced, and enjoyed in numerous aspects of life—medicine, work, entertainment, lifestyle, transportation—but were not *seen or known* when it came to the nation's military and warfare matters. Scientific and military advancements were made at the "sub" level and, like the nuclear cosmos in which they originated, they literally embodied the characteristics of invisibility and restricted elite access. In fact, the Manhattan Project was so well buried that it was not until 13 days after the death of President Roosevelt on April 12, 1945, that his successor, (Vice) President Truman was first briefed about the MED and the capabilities nuclear weapons technologies harbored (Kelly, 2007, p. 464). Ironically, it was FDR who had nurtured the project for six years, but it would be Truman who signed the executive orders and authorized the use of atomic weapons against Japan less than four months into his first term as president. Regrettably, the formalized protest *Franck Report* was to no avail and the *Petition to the President of the United States* from nuclear scientists and others in the MED community was not delivered to President Truman; these inactions signify another facet of the immense secrecy surrounding the MED's shadow.

On August 6, 1945, the B-29 Bomber *Enola Gay* departed on its mission toward Hiroshima, Japan, with orders for the crew to fire upon the city only if they had plain eyesight of their primary target. At 8:15 a.m., the first atomic uranium bomb, named Little Boy, was dropped without proper warning through clear skies over Hiroshima—a time when the maximum number of the civilian populace was most likely to be outside of their homes and commuting for their Monday work or school day. Nearly 80,000 civilians were killed instantly (Kelly, 2007, p. 330). Sixteen hours after its detonation, President Truman and Secretary of War Stimson informed the American public about the secret bomb in a glut of radio announcements and newspaper articles (Kelly, 2007, pp. 317–318):

> on the day of the destruction of Hiroshima the floodgates of official publicity were swung wide. Rivers of racy material prepared in our various agencies of Public Enlightenment poured out to the press and radio commentators whose well-understood duty is to "condition" public opinions. Puddles of ink confusedly outlined the techniques whereby we have successfully broken the Laws of God.
>
> (Morley, 2007, p. 400)

Two days later the Soviet Union declared war on Japan; on August 9, 1945 the U.S. dropped a second and more destructive plutonium nuclear bomb, Fat Man, on Nagasaki, Japan killing and wounding 75,000 (Yamazaki, n.d.); and six days later Japan surrendered to the Allied Powers (Kelly, 2007; Bird & Lifschultz, 1998).

Following six years of meticulous and pedantic planning, the U.S.'s cultural secret officially detonated upon the world's stage, twice searing the mushroom cloud image into the collective consciousness, and thrusting our hidden shadow potentials out into the open. Our Promethean hubris, which, a few years prior, unlocked the thermonuclear universe for a select elite's utilization, had a second and perhaps more important discovery as well—we definitively knew as a human race that we possessed the potential to self-destruct, and to mass annihilate human life and sentient beings on the planet earth. With this earth-shattering realization, the collective's psychological response enters *enantiodromia* which is the depth psychological focus of Part II.

References

Archer Productions Incorporated (Producer). (1951). *Duck and cover* [Official Civil Defense Film]. United States: Federal Civil Defense Administration. Retrieved from www.youtube.com/watch?v= IKqXu-5jw60

Bird, K., & Lifschultz, L. (Eds.). (1998). *Hiroshima's shadow: Writings on the denial of history and the Smithsonian controversy*. Stonycreek, CT: Pamphleteer's Press.

Brodie, B. (Ed.). (1946). *The absolute weapon: Atomic power and world order*. New York, NY: Harcourt, Brace and Co.

Dahl, P. F. (1999). *Heavy water and the wartime race for nuclear energy*. Bristol, England: Taylor & Francis.

Edinger, E. (1999). *Archetype of the apocalypse: A Jungian study of the book of Revelation*. Chicago, IL: Open Court.

Federation of American Scientists (n.d.). The Franck report. Retrieved from www.fas.org/sgp/eprint/franck.html

Gaimon, N., Grant, A., & Verheiden, M. (1989). *Secret origins special #1: Batman's best villains: The Riddler, Two-Face, and the Penguin*. New York, NY: Random House.

Giegerich, W. (2007). *Technology and the soul: From the nuclear bomb to the world wide web*. New Orleans, LA: Spring Journal Books.

Hillman, J. (2004). *A terrible love of war*. New York, NY: The Penguin Press.

Hopcke, R. H. (1999). *A guided tour of the collected works of C. G. Jung*. Boston, MA: Shambhala.

Jung, C. G. (1959). *Aion*. Princeton, NJ: Princeton University Press.

Jung, C. G. (1961). *Memories, dreams, reflections*. New York, NY: Vintage Books.

Jung, C. G. (1978). *Flying saucers: A modern myth of things seen in the skies*. New York, NY: MJF Books.

Jung, C. G. (1981). *Archetypes and the collective unconscious*. Princeton, NJ: Princeton University Press.

Kelly, C. C. (2007). *The Manhattan Project: The birth of the atomic bomb in the words of its creators, eyewitnesses, and historians*. New York, NY: Black Dog & Leventhal.

Maguire, G. (1995). *Wicked: The life and times of the wicked witch of the west*. New York, NY: Harper Collins.

May, R. (1991). *The cry for myth*. New York, NY: Dell.

Miller, W. A. (1989). *Your golden shadow: Discovering and fulfilling your undeveloped self*. San Francisco, CA: Harper & Row.

Morley, F. (2007). The return to nothingness. In C. Kelly (Ed.), *The Manhattan Project: The birth of the atomic bomb in the words of its creators, eyewitnesses, and historians* (pp. 399–400). New York, NY: Black Dog & Leventhal.

Nichols, K. D. (2007). The biggest S.O.B. In C. Kelly (Ed.), *The Manhattan Project: The birth of the atomic bomb in the words of its creators, eyewitnesses, and historians* (p. 121). New York, NY: Black Dog & Leventhal.

Norris, R. S. (2007). Unprecedented security measures. In C. Kelly (Ed.), *The Manhattan Project: The birth of the atomic bomb in the words of its creators, eyewitnesses, and historians* (pp. 233–235). New York, NY: Black Dog & Leventhal.

Poe, E. A. (1983). *The tell-tale heart and other writings.* New York, NY: Bantam Dell.

Romanyshyn, R. D. (1989). *Technology as symptom and dream.* New York, NY: Brunner-Routledge.

Rotblat, J., & Ikeda, D. (2007). *A quest for global peace: Rotblat and Ikeda on war, ethics, and the nuclear threat.* New York, NY: I.B. Tauris.

Rowling, J. K. (2004). *Harry Potter and the order of the phoenix.* New York, NY: Scholastic Inc.

Samuels, A. (1993). *The political psyche.* New York, NY: Routledge.

Samuels, A., Shorter, B., & Plaut, F. (1986). *A critical dictionary of Jungian analysis.* New York, NY: Routledge.

Sanford, J. A. (1991). Dr. Jekyll and Mr. Hyde. In C. Zweig & J. Abrams (Eds.), *Meeting the shadow: The hidden power of the dark side of human nature* (pp. 29–34). New York, NY: Jeremy Tarcher/Penguin.

Schweber, S. S. (2000). *In the shadow of the bomb: Bethe, Oppenheimer, and the moral responsibility of the scientist.* Princeton, NJ: Princeton University Press.

Shakespeare, W. (1993). *Othello.* New York, NY: Washington Square Press.

Shaw, G. B., & Lerner, A. J. (2006). *Pygmalion and my fair lady.* New York, NY: Penguin Putnam.

Shelley, M. (2011). *Frankenstein.* New York, NY: SoHo Books.

Singer, T. (Ed.) (2000). *The vision thing: Myth, politics and psyche in the world.* New York, NY: Routledge.

Singer, T., & Kimbles, S. L. (Eds.) (2004). *The cultural complex: Contemporary Jungian perspectives on psyche and society.* New York, NY: Routledge.

Stein, M. (1998). *Jung's map of the soul.* Chicago, IL: Open Court.

Stevens, A. (1999). *On Jung: An updated edition with a reply to Jung's critics.* Princeton, NJ: Princeton University Press.

Stevenson, R. L. (2008). *The strange case of Dr. Jekyll and Mr. Hyde and other tales.* New York, NY: Oxford University Press.

Storr, A. (1983). *The essential Jung: Selected writings.* Princeton, NJ: Princeton University Press.
Tanaka, T. (Producer), & Honda, I. (Director). (1954). *Gojira* [DVD]. Tokyo: Toho Film Company, Ltd.
US Inflation Calculator (n.d.). Retrieved January 8, 2023 from www.usinflationcalculator.com/
Van Eenwyk, J. R. (1997). *Archetypes and strange attractors: The chaotic world of symbols.* Toronto: Inner City Books.
Welles, O. (1938, October). War of the Worlds: Mercury Theater original radio broadcast. Retrieved from www.loc.gov/static/programs/national-recording-preservation-board/documents/TheWaroftheWorlds.pdf
Wendt, G., & Geddes, D. P. (Eds.). (1945). *The atomic age opens.* Cleveland, OH: World Publishing.
Wilde, O. (1998). *The picture of Dorian Gray.* New York, NY: Random House.
Yamazaki, J. N. (n.d.). Hiroshima and Nagasaki death toll: Children of the atomic bomb. Retrieved from www.aasc.ucla.edu/cab/200708230009.html
Zweig, C., & Abrams, J. (Eds.). (1991). *Meeting the shadow: The hidden power of the dark side of human nature.* New York, NY: Jeremy Tarcher/Penguin.

Part II: Enantiodromia
RadioActive Psyche

The atomic bomb is not the only thing to detonate onto the world stage in August 1945; a nuclearized consciousness forcibly mushrooms alongside it and produces a widespread radioactive psyche that is particularly reactive during the years of 1945–1958 (some may argue that it continues to be to this day with ongoing nonproliferation international relations treaties and policies). *Enantiodromia* or, in its most simplistic understanding, the reversal of a psychic situation, commences shortly after the fallout of entering the atomic age settles. The radioactive era of duck and cover drills, UFOs, *Godzilla*, and underground fallout shelters rushes in to help the collective process and contain the atomic age's tangible threat to the survival of all living organisms and its ensuing psychological chaos.

As we'll see in Part III, this churning enantiodromian chaos becomes the drive for an eventual critical mass of influential British citizens to come together, organize against their government's atomic weapons programs, and birth the ND image/peace symbol and its associated movements. For now, however, and because it sets the stage for what is to come, we will investigate the depth psychological perspective of enantiodromia to understand how this process evolves at the collective levels.

Psychological Enantiodromia

The traditional concept of *enantiodromia*, the reversal of one extreme into its opposite (Samuels, 2000), is not a Jungian innovation, but rather an aged idea in Buddhism, Islam, and Christianity, as well as myriad philosophy traditions and in paradigm specific law-of-opposites, such as the law of equilibrium or homeostasis (see Figure 2.1). Finding utility for this concept in psychoanalysis, Jung likely constructed his theory on pre-Socratic Greek philosopher Heraclitus' ideations, and his unique contribution to the enduring concept is the psychological approach, that "certain mental processes are turned at a given point into their opposite as if through a kind of self-regulation" (Ellenberger, 1970, p. 713). For psychoanalytically informed circles, this perspective is significant for understanding individuals and groups at different psychological registers and scales.

For instance, Jung suggests that the "individual shadow contains within it the seed of an enantiodromia, of a conversion into its opposite" (Van Eenwyk, 1997, p. 93). Samuels (2000) hints that the clinical psychological principle of the *wounded healer* is based in enantiodromia. Perhaps Romanyshyn (2007) would likewise hint at an enantiodromian base for his *wounded researcher* principle, and in a February 26, 2011 interview named "America and the Shift in Ages" for the *Huffington Post* Internet newspaper, James Hillman offered his take on the times, "a very old idea is at work behind our current state of affairs: enantiodromia, or the Greek notion of things turning into their opposite."

A popular Eurocentric literary occurrence of enantiodromia is allegorized in Dante Alighieri's *The Divine Comedy* (trans. 1995). When Dante and Virgil descend to the most frigid depths of hell, and then rebound in a reverse path toward the realms of purgatory and heaven, they experience enantiodromia, described as a mysterious and spontaneous regression, or the characteristic

Figure 2.1 Uroborus. Credit: Matthew C. Clonch.

feature of "any journey through the unconscious" (Ellenberger, 1970, p. 713). So important to depth psychology is the process to journey through the unconscious that it eventually becomes a distinguishing "feature of Jungian synthetic-hermeneutic therapy" (p. 713). However, a better-suited literary example is the myth of the goddess Inanna-Ishtar, as interpreted by Sylvia Brinton Perera (1981). She illuminates the concept of enantiodromia via woman-centered mythologems of "descent and return. ...a model for health and for healing the split between above and below, between the collective ideal and the powerful bipolar, transformative, processual reality underlying the feminine wholeness pattern" (p. 94). Perera's statement intimates that healing occurs in the overlapping nexus of two poles, the *balancing* between one realm and another, and emphasizes wholeness; this position is significant to our investigation of enantiodromia and we will return to it in just a moment.

In *Technology and the Soul: From the Nuclear Bomb to the World Wide Web*, Giegerich (2007) similarly applies a modified notion of enantiodromia to the nuclear age, but does not name it as such. He observes:

> With the explicit appearance from outside of the inner *telos* of our collective doings, and with the Bomb's throwing us back onto ourselves, a reversal takes place, similar to one occurring with the appearance of the neurotic symptom in the individual. Now we have become the victims instead of the doers, but in such a way that it becomes apparent in our doings we had all along been the victims of what was driving us.
>
> (p. 64)

Giegerich's reliance on the concept of interdependence is vital. Although he frames it within the patriarchal notions of victor and vanquished, he suggests that they coexist in any given moment, that their intensities determine whether one is figure while the other is ground, and both are necessary for a complete gestalt.

The prevailing and orthodox perspective of enantiodromia, however, rests upon a bifurcated and fixed model that positions two notions as oppositional, adaptive or maladaptive, overly determined mechanisms that simply reverse in form from one into the other; that one incarnation of an experience must withdraw completely from Point A in order to reappear as its opposite experience at Point B, as if it were a linear process, or a pendulum swinging where the visible form at the peak of its bob is indicative of the location of its sum total mechanical energy. In the context of depth psychological frameworks such as ego and shadow, light and dark, transcendence and descent, adaptive behaviors and defense mechanisms, healthy and pathological functioning, where the presence of one indicates the absence of the other, this approach makes sense.

At the same time, this position needs fine-tuning to best serve a peace-centered inquiry that rejects as its premise the naive definition of peace as the "absence of war;" a definition that conveniently undermines the deeply complex delivery and infancy of the nascent atomic age. Perera and Giegerich's pluralistic approaches are more in line with my understanding of the notion of enantiodromia, and as such enantiodromia is imagined as more of a liminal and overlapping "twilight" rather than an efficient split transition from "day's light" to "night's darkness." Applying the notion of interdependence to enantiodromia opens up the otherwise pooling psychological energy to the inherent possibilities available in the collective psychological landscape. It allows for multiple and incongruous psychological processes to be present and working within psyche at any given time.

The Atomic Age Opens

While feverishly guarding against espionage infiltration, the top secret atomic age commenced when the first clandestine atomic test bomb, nicknamed "the Gadget," detonated for the first time under the code name "Trinity Test" in the deserts of Alamogordo, New Mexico at 5:30 am on July 16, 1945 by scientists of the Los Alamos Laboratory under the direction of J. Robert Oppenheimer (Kelly, 2007; Schweber, 2000). Approximately four weeks later and within days of the atomic bombs detonating over Hiroshima and Nagasaki—which effectively slingshot the Manhattan Project's secret into the collective consciousness—the publisher Pocket Books coined the terms *atomic age* and *nuclear age* when they printed a special primer, edited by Gerald Wendt and Donald P. Geddes, titled *The Atomic Age Opens* (Wendt & Geddes, 1945; Kramer, 2005).

According to Kramer (2005), the term *atomic age* was more popular throughout the early and mid-1950s, although the term *nuclear age* was used early in locations of authority, such as in the name of physics textbooks, and by the late 1950s it became the preferred neologism. The following passage from the above-mentioned introduction of *The Atomic Age Opens* (Wendt & Geddes, 1945), was widely available to the U.S. population by the end of August 1945. It intended to appeal to and to edify the general public about nuclear power and technologies, its synthetic and natural manufacture, and its "omnipresent and inexhaustible" supply, and also to show "the nature and extent of public reaction to this astounding discovery" (p. 10). The text is a succinct and well-written summary of this extraordinary world-history event and, unlike other reports or bulletins of the day, which relied on authoritative points of view from physicists, military officials, or government administrators, this work was written by an author who, although a noted academician and member of the American Humanist Association, writes in lay language from the perspective of an ethical culturalist. Titled *Man Had Divided the Indivisible*, Gerald Wendt's own experience and framing of this new epoch for the Western collective in its first few weeks of nascency is useful, and thus a sizeable portion is included here, aiming to provide the reader with his unmediated perspective on the neonate nuclear problematic:

> Now this basic force, this secret of the sun, this energy beyond all comprehension, this power to revolutionize man's way of living, has been found. The indivisible atom has been split, and mankind stands at the threshold of a future no one can foresee. The scientists have given us a new world in which there will be order or chaos as we will have it. The chaos will be easily obtainable; in fact it will be inevitable if this new force is not controlled by a new sense of social responsibility that will equal the dangers. Man is no longer playing with Chinese firecrackers which at the worst can only burn local fingers and start isolated fires. He is now beginning a road that may take him to a point where he can harness the sun to do his bidding... ..
>
> The nuclear physicists have opened the Atomic Age and have thereby imposed upon every thinking human being—not just upon sociologists and politicians—the vital necessity of

making those adjustments in thinking, in laws, in ways of life, in human relationships, that will prevent the chaos and give mankind instead a future golden and peaceful.
(Wendt & Geddes, pp. 9–10)

Within weeks of the ultra-secret Manhattan Project's unveiling, the archetypal and mythological underpinnings of the atomic age's dawn were clear. Wendt alludes to humans mastering nature in a nod to the Prometheus myth, discovering the source of the sun's energy, overcoming the herculean task of splitting the indivisible atom, and standing at the crossroads with the power to decide embarkation of either a chaotic or peaceful *new world*. In the spirit of similarly inquiring into some of the "adjustments in thinking, in laws, in ways of life, in human relationships" that Wendt points at above, the remainder of Part II will focus on the pivotal years of 1945–1957. Please note that from this point forward, we will use today's more colloquially familiar term *nuclear age* instead of *atomic age*.

Modern Day Prometheus?

Prior to the detonations of Little Boy and Fat Man over Japan, anthropogenic radioactive contamination did not significantly interfere with atmospheric, ecological, food chain, or food web systems. After the August 6th and August 9th radiation, poisoning lumbered through the atmosphere and nuclear fallout settled onto the earth, it seems that radiation leaked not only into these and other worldwide systems (such as politics and economics), but also into our collective psychological schemas, producing a kind of "radioactive psyche" underlying the collective consciousness. For the first time we, the collective human race, were forced to acknowledge that we now had the bona fide power to permanently destroy our earth and ourselves—a power previously reserved only for God, gods, or other higher powers. We indeed reached an original apex of human consciousness, and in response we appropriated the proverbial "Promethean fire," holding it above our heads as we entered the nuclear age with it as our torch. From 1945 until 1948, the U.S. and Britain monopolized nuclear weapons intelligence; in 1949 the Soviet Union conducted their first test, with France and China adding to nuclear proliferation before the end of the nuclear age's second decade (Reed & Stillman, 2010).

The Prometheus myth is central for this story as it scales both the individual and collective levels, and although there are several versions of the succession myth throughout antiquity, Hesiod's version from *Theogony* (trans. 1993), is the one referenced. From an appreciative perspective, the archetypal figure of Prometheus is a champion and benefactor of the human race, credited with gifting fire to humankind and establishing sacrificial norms. From a contrary perspective, Prometheus is a trickster figure amongst the Greek Titans, one who is not to be trusted and one who upsets the existing cosmic order in two ways. First, he stole the divine fire secret from Zeus's thunderbolt and presented it to ordinary mortals, and second, he made a mockery of Zeus, using deception and covers, to swindle him into eating an inedible sacrificial offering, thus overturning established sacrificial rites and re-establishing sacrificial norms advantageous to mortals and disadvantageous to the gods. Zeus punished him by chaining him to a mountain, and having an eagle (one of his shapeshifting emblems) eat his insides out each day. Because Prometheus is immortal, his internal organs regenerated each night, thus perpetuating his punishment with each rising dawn.

Oppenheimer, who was astutely aware of the repercussions of introducing nuclear weapons to the world, addressed the assembled groups of the National Academy of Sciences and the American Philosophical Society a few months after the bombings of Japan, saying, "the atomic bomb constituted 'a vast new threat, and a new one, to all people of the earth, by its novelty, its terror, [and] its strangely promethean quality'" (Schweber, 2000, p.11). We can infer from his words that Oppenheimer understood that he himself was in a unique position, perhaps even embodying a modern human facsimile of Prometheus, for we could insert his name in the above description of Prometheus' myth and it would be suitable for the scientific director of the Manhattan Project: *From an appreciative perspective, Oppenheimer is a champion and benefactor of the human race, credited with gifting nuclear weapons—ceasing the long and sufferable great world war—and establishing new sacrificial war norms. From a contrary perspective, Oppenheimer is a trickster figure amongst the WWII Titans, one who is not to be trusted and one who upsets the existing cosmic order in two ways. First, he stole the atomic fire secret from the gods and presented it to ordinary politicians and military personnel....* and so on and so forth.

Interestingly, in Oppenheimer's lifetime, President Eisenhower (a Zeus figure in 1950s U.S. politics) dismissed his governmental clearance, and the Atomic Energy Commission asked him to resign from his position as Chairman of its General Advisory Committee. A target of McCarthyism, Oppenheimer was investigated by the House Un-American Activities Committee, was "pecked at" during his Congressional trial (a personification of an American eagle), and was professionally shunned, resulting in a self-imposed exile to the island of St. John in the Caribbean (Bird & Sherwin, 2005). One further parallel between Prometheus and Oppenheimer: Oppenheimer's moral positions and cautions against nuclear weapon technologies are well documented in his speeches and writings from the last 20 years of his life. The consequences of introducing nuclear technologies into international politics gnawed at him, weighed on his mind, catalyzed him to speak up and against them, *and* singularly chained him to this one mountainous achievement of his professional career.

Nuclear Paranoia and Fallout

Remember the image of the bottle imp Mercurius exploding "out of the bottle and tak[ing] on tremendous proportions, threatening to kill its liberator" (Giegerich, 2007, p. 102)? It is a metaphor for both the American ego and shadow, the glass vessel that contains and seals off our mercurial shadow drives and instincts. The ego was—and continues to be—substantial and thick which, in Jungian psychoanalytics, assures us that its psychological equivalent, the shadow, is equally massive and steeped with its own nefarious or underdeveloped potentials. In the immediate aftermath of Hiroshima and Nagasaki, proponents of the bomb anxiously worked to preserve the American ego, the cracked glass vessel, in the face of growing dissension from within the U.S. and from around the world. Hyperrationalization of Truman's decision and justifications for using the bomb frequently relied on soldiers' experiences to churn up patriotic affect within the general U.S. public. One notable article, Paul Fussell's "Thank God for the Atom Bomb," capitalizes on this technique and implores from a soldier's point of view, "we broke down and cried with relief and joy. We were going to live. We were going to grow to adulthood afterall...when the *Enola Gay* dropped its package, 'there were cheers'" (1988, p. 397).

Roughly around the same time, however, and dipping into the same pool of churned-up collective affect, an article published in *Human Events* on August 29, 1945, suggests that our ego vessel had shattered and fear of its mercurial shadow contents "killing" its liberator were very real. Morley (2007) writes, "Never has any totalitarian propaganda effort fallen more flat. Instead of the anticipated wave of nationalistic enthusiasm, the general reaction was one of unconcealed horror" (p. 400). The unconcealed horror is the "expectation of retribution" from the enemy which, Morley pleads, "springs from consciousness of sin... . more important in this unease is the loss of individual dignity and spiritual peace—the consciousness of being hopelessly adrift; of having lost contact with those standards by which men really live" (p. 399). Fussell's and Morley's articles imply that a transitioning collective consciousness required a distention of itself in order to contain the rising internal pressure from the mixed feelings, morals, and logical debates surrounding the differing positions on the nuclear problematic. These intense post-Bomb experiences, or psychological shadow encounters, would be akin to what Zweig and Abrams (1991) call "meeting our demons, wrestling with the devil, descent to the underworld, and dark night of the soul" (p. 3).

Therefore, in the post-1945 psychological landscape—where a shifting of its parameters began when the collective consciousness learned of its nuclear-injected shadow potentials, where it wrestled with intense affect such as fear, paranoia, and anxiety, and grappled with new moral implications of its own invention—we will see the public imaginary's attempt to expand its existing matrix by creating new locations and containers of consciousness. According to Dwight, Boler, and Sears (2006), "the public imaginary shapes in part what is possible. The public imaginary—the conscious and unconscious, collectively shared cultural myths structured by popular discourses of advertising and Hollywood—is saturated with images that reinforce stereotyped narratives of social roles" (p. 1467). Part I discussed several of the prevailing myths and public discourses that allowed for and enabled the Manhattan Project's copious underground development—the Manifest Destiny, Apocalyptic fears, the lure of the fantasized frontier. Now we'll include the public imaginary discourses of the entertainment industry, science fiction, and government apparatuses such as the Federal Civil Defense Administration (FCDA) (the predecessor to today's Federal Emergency Management Agency [FEMA]) that enabled the public to morally, emotionally, and psychologically wrestle with the gargantuan questions raised by the atomic bomb's materialization.

Depending on their propagandized slant, the government and media articulated or provided a host of nuclear visualities for the general public through firsthand accounts, eyewitness and news reports, photojournalism, and video footage that proffered either the benefits of an international deterrence security system (ego) or unimaginable nuclear horrors (shadow). Soon, they labored to offset what was becoming a groundswell of fear and anxiety around basic survival needs and perpetuation of the human race. Lorenz and Watkins' (2003) discussion of percepticide, "when whole populations are forced to not-know what is going on around them... . watching-with-out-seeing... . this kind of renunciation establishes a split within the self, where certain knowings are exiled and unavailable for the negotiation of one's life" (p. 14), is especially poignant in the early years of the nuclear age when the government was in strict control of nuclear technologies, nuclear tropes, images, discourses, and international security measures. To frame as a repeated crime against humanity the U.S.'s decision to use nuclear warfare technology against Japan would not only jeopardize the average citizen's ego-friendly patriotic sense of duty, but also directly confront and affirm the proximity of the U.S.'s vast shadow nature. To this end, a few key and accessible cultural artifacts that specifically respond to the formative years of nuclear age are utilized by the government and lay industries to manage the intensifying and pooling affect—starting with the FCDA public service film *Duck and Cover*, moving to the film industry's take on the unpredictable nuclear age, and then rotating toward the proliferation of circular cultural artifacts that functioned to mediate collective affect during this time.

RadioActive Psyche: *Duck and Cover*, *Godzilla*, UFOs, and Fallout Shelters

Two years after the Soviet Union commenced the Cold War by joining the nuclear arms race, the 1951 U.S. FCDA short public service film, *Duck and Cover* (Archer Productions), was used primarily in school classrooms to instruct a generation of students in personal protection against a possible imminent nuclear attack. Employing a mix of cartoons, a memorable jingle, and stock video during the nine-minute film, the authoritarian voice of the male narrator repeatedly affirms to the child viewer that they "know what to do" when they see a brilliant flash of light and that we all know how to "save ourselves" if "the atomic bomb is used against us." The continuous references to an attack being imminent, that "it could happen at any time," that children should always be ready to "duck and cover" whether they are in their classroom, enjoying a family picnic, working on the farm, or riding their bikes down the street, instills, and at the same time produces, a state of perpetual generalized anxiety in both children and adults alike.

Once the film sets the anxiety threat in motion, thereby inciting the viewer's survival instinct, the narrator quickly assures the viewer that because the FCDA has taught them how to identify a nuclear attack, how to protect themselves and others, how to enlist an adult's help if they are not sure what to do, that they can rest assured that the government does indeed have a plan of protection for each of its citizens called "Duck and Cover." Entrusting the children with knowledge of the government's "Duck and Cover" security plan sends the message that they too can be an essential helper of the necessary political and ethical order, not of the ensuing chaos, to outlast the nuclear bomb and its radiation.

Likewise, the rhetorical device of *aestheticization*, or the presentation of "a dynamic image of the world that is curiously both volatile and stable, in which periodic explosions into disorder are always brought somehow back under control" (Spurr, 2004, p. 44) becomes part of the narrative repair function of *Duck and Cover*. The public service script outlines a return from social insecurity and crisis to resolution that is brought forth from the official authority of the FCDA. In this way, the film establishes "a subtle relation between narrative order and the perception or representation of political order" (p. 44). Indeed, the appearance of a calm and controlled federal government was a primary objective at a time when the collective was still recoiling from the initial nuclear crisis of 1945 and was now confronted with fears stemming from the budding Cold War crisis. Ultimately, the government's purpose here is to encourage viewers to feel safe in their neighborhoods as long as they "know what to do"; this allows the government to feel more at ease because they have taken measures to manage the collective's escalating affect.

Feeling safe in one's own neighborhood became a central feature of 1950s tidy television shows such as *I Love Lucy (1951–1957)*, *The Adventures of Ozzie and Harriet (1952–1966)*, and *Father Knows Best (1954–1960)*. The theme of aestheticization was followed closely by showcasing composed storylines with a minor disorder flare-up that was easily brought under control, just as the FDCA did in its materials. This too happens in films such as *An American in Paris (1951)*, *Singin' in the Rain (1952)*, and *From Here to Eternity (1953)* where presenting alternative social narratives and cultural myths is the magic ingredient of Hollywood. And while science fiction motion pictures had only a few key cinematic successes in the first half of the 20th century with 1931's *Frankenstein* and 1933's *King Kong*, the genre came into its own in the 1950s—and for good reason.

When thermonuclear advancements procured the ability to split the "indivisible atom" into two, initial understandings implied that the split also bore twin products: progressive and beneficial power, and chaotic and destructive power (Wendt & Geddes, 1945, p. 9). The general public did not have much voice in the nuclear matter, nor did they have real agency to engage, act, or vote on the nuclear matter. It was an overwhelming and overburdening problematic to consider. One accessible technique the general public could easily use to assuage the generalized feelings of fear and anxiety was to immerse and ground the senses in a cinematically based pleasure principle experience. Thus, science fiction became a genre of narrative repair that offered a distant and safe place on which the public imaginary could project multitudinal possibilities into the future. The genre became known for its interesting cross sections between temporalities, mythologies, eschatologies, cosmologies, alternative histories, advancing technologies, and motifs such as space exploration (unknown territories) and surprise and deadly alien invasions. This last topic is significant, particular for the West. Where else have we before heard of mass annihilation attacks without proper warning?

After the 1952 hydrogen bomb tests off of Bikini Atoll in the Pacific Islands, which were approximately 1,000 times more destructive than the atomic bombs detonated on Hiroshima and Nagasaki (Bird & Lifschulz, 1998), the public imaginary struggled with increasing amounts of fear and anxiety and began sublimating its radioactive affect into the container of radioactive cinema. In 1954, Tanaka and Honda of the Toho Film Company of Japan released the first significant creature feature film of the nuclear age, *Gojira* and in 1956, the American version *Godzilla: King of the Monsters* was released in theaters to blockbuster success. As mentioned before, Gojira is the Japanese mythological ocean creature that absorbs the hydrogen bomb radioactive byproducts in Tokyo Bay, mutates, reawakens from a 1,000-year hibernation to cause indiscriminate mass destruction in Japan and is defeated shortly thereafter by Japanese ingenuity.

The Anglicized Godzilla is not an exact reproduction of Gojira and is therefore problematic in that the Japanese narrative is interrupted and manipulated, left out are important narrative details that implicate the West, the protagonist role no longer belongs to a Japanese citizen but to a white male American reporter, and its parataxic approach undermines the haunting nuclear narrative from the Japanese viewpoint. The colonialist revisioning of the Japanese narrative is readily apparent even in the minutia of descriptor tags given by Netflix to both films; *Gojira* is tagged as "controversial" and "dark," while *Godzilla: King of the Monsters* is tagged as "campy" and "exciting."

In *Immortal Monster: The Mythological Evolution of the Fantastic Beast in Modern Fiction and Film*, Andriano (1999) writes

> These fantastic beasts were long thought to represent the monstrous Other we feared yet found fascinating. But at least since Freud's time, we have come to know the monster as a projection of some repressed part of the Self. Whether repressed id, shadow, animus, anima, instinct, or impulse from the reptile brain; whether oppressed race or extirpated species, the uncanny monster is the familiar Self disguised as the alien Other. Sometimes conquered (like King Kong) but often unvanquished (like Moby-Dick), these monsters never seem to die. Even the ones that appear to die in the end of their tales come back to haunt us in sequels, adaptations, remakes, and parodies.

We need this monster to define ourselves, because we have always known that the Mark of the Beast is our own signature.

(p. xi)

If we heed Andriano's conclusions, it is easy to understand why there is a superfluity of *Godzilla* (and outsized friends) sequels spawning generations of science fiction films. As we continue to live with the bomb, we continue to need a culturally relevant, accessible, and safe place to work out our fears about nuclear contamination or annihilation, to work out our anxieties around life with the bomb, to create innovative solutions to our problems, or to rewrite or imagine different and alternatives histories and futures for ourselves and our descendants.

In 1947, about nine years before *Godzilla* hit movie theaters, and just two years after the nuclear attacks on Japan, widespread cultural attention turned toward the profusion of reported Unidentified Flying Objects (UFOs). These objects were also known as *flying saucers* or *flying discs*, and while initially reported widely in the West, eyewitness reports began surfacing in record numbers all around the globe (Jung, 1978). From a psychological point of view, Jung was deeply interested in the UFO phenomenon, wrote extensively on the topic, and mused over the God-image possibilities circular symbols hold and represent. From this springboard, he reflected upon the present cultural milieu where a "profound dichotomy" between the sacred and profane

> penetrates even into world politics, [and in response] a compensation has arisen. This takes the form of circular symbols of unity which represent a synthesis of opposites within the psyche. I refer to the worldwide rumors of Unidentified Flying Objects.
>
> (p. 334)

Symbols, according to Jung, are an "unconscious invention in answer to a conscious problematic" (Samuels, Shorter & Plaut, 1986, p. 146).

Building upon Jung's observations on the UFO phenomenon, the proliferation of radiation warning signs and fallout shelter signs of the late 1940s–1960s (see Figure 2.2) might also represent an unconscious collective compensation for wholeness, unity, and survival during a time when the risk of physical and psychic destruction was real. If the signs are understood through a mandala lens, they may have served to "produce an inner order—which is why," Jung states, "when they appear in a series, they often follow chaotic, disordered states marked by conflict and anxiety. They express the idea of a refuge, of inner reconciliation and wholeness" (1969, p. 100). While the signs' genesis are exclusive from one another (the radiation warning sign was created informally in 1946 [Frame, n.d.] and the FCDA formally created the fallout shelter sign in 1961 [Oak Ridge Associated Universities, n.d.]), circular imagery resonates diachronously throughout the years post-1945; we see it in the designs of a host of additional circular FCDA insignias and emblems, as well as in the emergence of the circular CND image in 1958. Indeed, there appears to be a serial chronology of circular image appearances—1946: radiation warning sign; 1947: UFOs; 1951: reissue of circular FCDA emblems, logos, and insignias; 1958: ND/Peace image; and 1961: fallout shelter signs, to name but a few.

According to Paul Frame (n.d.), of the Oak Ridge Institute for Science and Education, the radiation warning sign (Figure 2.2) was casually scribbled by laboratory scientists at the University of California-Berkeley in 1946, the year following the nuclear detonations over Hiroshima and Nagasaki. He notes several popularized speculations as to why that particular design was

Figure 2.2 Radiation Warning and Fallout Shelter Signs. Credit: Matthew C. Clonch.

Enantiodromia 47

chosen—(a) that the small center circle signifies an atom with three "blades," or "atomic energy radiating out," representing three different types of radiation particles—alpha, beta, and gamma; (b) that someone saw a similar graphic being used at a naval base dry dock to warn of spinning propellers; and (c) that the sign has similarities to the enemy Japanese battle flag of WWII which would have been quite familiar to West Coast inhabitants (Frame's own speculation), (see Figure 2.3).

The fallout shelter sign, however, was designed by the FCDA and introduced to the public in December 1961 (Oak Ridge Associated Universities, n.d.). Originally, the FCDA wanted fallout shelters to use the radiation warning sign, but "this idea was rejected because a fallout shelter represents safety whereas the radiation warning symbol represents a hazard" (Oak Ridge Associated Universities, n.d.). Recognizing the psychological underpinnings inherent in images, and the government's need to communicate their civil defense message clearly, the FCDA awarded the contract for the sign's design to graphic arts studios and

> designated [that] the services of a psychologist be obtained to recommend a visual symbol that could be easily identified and remembered. The sign had to meet the psychological requirements of simplicity, easy identification, retention, and arresting color combination.
>
> It had to be simple enough to be easily identified by children, non-English speaking persons or others who may not be able to read. The color combination, yellow and black, is considered as the most easily identified attention getter by psychologists in

Figure 2.3 Japanese Battle Flag WWII. Credit: Matthew C. Clonch.

the graphic arts industry. The sign can be seen and recognized at distances up to 200 feet.

The shelter symbol on the sign is a black circle set against a yellow rectangular background. Inside the circle, three yellow triangles are arranged in geometric pattern with apex of the triangle pointing down.

(Oak Ridge Associated Universities, n.d.)

If we again look with a mandala lens at the fallout shelter sign, we see that the three yellow triangles and the black encapsulating circle represent four distinct parts of the image. Jung (1969) writes that "the division of the mandala into four denotes a process of becoming conscious" (p. 38); to what exactly the collective was becoming conscious of in 1961 is hard to say, although we are aware of the psychological enantiodromian processes present in the collective consciousness when the fallout shelter sign debuts in the U.S. in 1961. It is worth mentioning that the fallout shelter signs occur several years after the CND image experiences remarkable success at Britain's protest marches, and 16 years after the bombings of Hiroshima and Nagasaki.

Lastly, in the above trilogy of signs of Figure 2.2 the second image is pertinent as it visually illustrates the concept of enantiodromia. On the left side is the radiation warning sign, and on the right is the fallout shelter sign. In the middle, however, the signs converge to create a composite of figure-and-ground, and we can see where the signs take their shape in the negative spaces of the graphic design of the other. The signs are strong and significant on their own, and do not necessarily suggest the absence of the other. And, yet, when they are brought together, we see that even though the fallout shelter sign is more prominent and foregrounded, the radiation warning sign is present despite its gray-scaled appearance in the background. In this composite configuration, they co-exist, are interdependent *and* independent, and point toward affiliated functions: One alerts us to the possibility of dangerous radiation in the area and the other alerts us to where we can find safety and protection from radiation.

The circular imagery of the radiation warning sign and the fallout shelter sign are stark reminders of the collective consciousness' inventiveness during the formative years of the nuclear age. Through these and numerous other cultural objects, the collective toiled through enantiodromian psychological processes and engaged with its mercurial affect through the creation of new locations and containers of consciousness. The (over)production of these circular images as a direct response to the nuclear age points toward the collective psyche's unconscious search for safety and protection. In 1957, the West's ability to deeply understand its power, voice, and agency in relation to nuclear matters reaches a critical point as a British grassroots group with an influential membership is meeting, discussing, and preparing to march themselves into the public nuclear disarmament (ND) discourse and to utilize the undeveloped constructive potentials mothballed in the collective shadow to gain worldwide attention. What eventually becomes known as the "Peace" social movement emerges in 1958 when the CND becomes a catalyst for a peace-full chain reaction of action and activism in the West.

References

Alighieri, D. (1995). *The divine comedy* (A. Mandelbaum, Trans.). New York, NY: Alfred A. Knopf.

Andriano, J. D. (1999). *Immortal monster: The mythological evolution of the fantastic beast in modern fiction and film.* Westport, CT: Greenwood Press.

Archer Productions Incorporated (Producer). (1951). *Duck and cover* [Official Civil Defense Film]. United States: Federal Civil Defense Administration. Retrieved from www.youtube.com/watch?v=IKqXu-5jw60

Bird, K., & Lifschultz, L. (Eds.). (1998). *Hiroshima's shadow: Writings on the denial of history and the Smithsonian controversy.* Stony Creek, CT: Pamphleteer's Press.

Bird, K., & Sherwin, M. J. (2005). *American Prometheus: The triumph and tragedy of J. Robert Oppenheimer.* New York, NY: Alfred A. Knopf.

Dwight, J. S., Boler, M., & Sears, P. (2006). Reconstructing the fables: Women on the educational cyberfrontier. *The International Handbook of Virtual Learning Environments, 1* (1), 1467–1494.

Ellenberger, H. F. (1970). *Discovery of the unconscious: The history and evolution of dynamic psychiatry.* New York, NY: Basic Books.

Frame, P. (n.d.). Radiation warning symbol (Trefoil). Retrieved from www.orau.org/health-physics-museum/collection/warning-signs/index.html

Fussell, H. (1988). *Thank God for the atom bomb and other essays.* New York, NY: Summit Books.

Giegerich, W. (2007). *Technology and the soul: From the nuclear bomb to the world wide web.* New Orleans, LA: Spring Journal Books.

Hesiod. (1993). *Works and days; Theogony* (S. Lombardo, Trans.). Indianapolis, IN: Hackett.

Hillman, J. (2011, February). America and the shift in ages: An interview with Jungian James Hillman. Retrieved from www.huffpost.com/entry/america-and-the-shift-in_b_822913

Jung, C. G. (1969). *Mandala symbolism.* Princeton, NJ: Princeton University Press.

Jung, C. G. (1978). *Flying saucers: A modern myth of things seen in the skies.* New York, NY: MJF Books.

Kelly, C. C. (2007). *The Manhattan Project: The birth of the atomic bomb in the words of its creators, eyewitnesses, and historians.* New York, NY: Black Dog & Leventhal.

Kramer, M. (2005). Nuclear age. In M. C. Horowitz (Ed.), *New dictionary of the history of ideas* (Vol. 4). (pp. 1646–1649). Detroit, MI: Charles Scribner's Sons.

Lorenz, H., & Watkins, M. (2003). Depth psychology and colonialism: Individuation, seeing-through, and liberation. *Quadrant, 33,* 11–32.

Morley, F. (2007). The return to nothingness. In C. Kelly (Ed.), *The Manhattan Project: The birth of the atomic bomb in the words of its creators, eyewitnesses, and historians* (pp. 399–400). New York, NY: Black Dog & Leventhal.

Oak Ridge Associated Universities (n.d.). Civil Defense Fallout Shelter Sign (ca. 1960s). Retrieved from www.orau.org/health-physics-museum/collection/civil-defense/miscellaneous/fallout.html

Perera, S. B. (1981). *Descent to the goddess: A way of initiation for women.* Toronto: Inner City Books.

Reed, T. C., & Stillman, D. B. (2010). *The nuclear express: A political history of the bomb and its proliferation.* Minneapolis, MN: Zenith Press.

Romanyshyn, R. D. (2007). *The wounded researcher: Research with soul in mind.* New Orleans, LA: Spring Journal Books.

Samuels, A. (2000). Post-Jungian dialogues. *Psychoanalytic Dialogues, 10* (3), 403–426. doi: http://dx.doi.org/10.1080/10481881009348555

Samuels, A., Shorter, B., & Plaut, F. (1986). *A critical dictionary of Jungian analysis.* New York, NY: Routledge.

Schweber, S. S. (2000). *In the shadow of the bomb: Bethe, Oppenheimer, and the moral responsibility of the scientist.* Princeton, NJ: Princeton University Press.

Spurr, D. (2004). *The rhetoric of empire: Colonial discourse in journalism, travel writing, and imperial administration.* Durham, NC: Duke.

Tanaka, T. (Producer), & Honda, I. (Director). (1954). *Gojira* [DVD]. Tokyo: Toho Film Company, Ltd.
Van Eenwyk, J. R. (1997). *Archetypes and strange attractors: The chaotic world of symbols.* Toronto: Inner City Books.
Wendt, G., & Geddes, D. P. (Eds.). (1945). *The atomic age opens.* Cleveland, OH: World Publishing.
Zweig, C., & Abrams, J. (Eds.). (1991). *Meeting the shadow: The hidden power of the dark side of human nature.* New York, NY: Jeremy Tarcher/Penguin.

Part III: Symbol

"A Human Being in Despair"

Instantly recognizable in most areas of the world as the "peace symbol" (see Figure 3.1), the simultaneously circular and forked British nuclear disarmament (ND) graphic was initially created as a basic marketing strategy for an ad-hoc Campaign for Nuclear Disarmament (CND)-sponsored 52-mile march from London's Trafalgar Square out to the small village of Aldermaston in April 1958. After the unpredictable success of the Aldermaston March, both the CND and the Direct Action Committee Against Nuclear War (DAC) adopted the ND graphic within a week's time to represent their respective organizations and their mutual ND goal (CND, 1958; Miles, 2008). Michael Randle (1986), a member of the Aldermaston March committee, recounts an unsympathetic reaction—probably reflective of many of the initial responses—to the campaign's adoption of the graphic:

> Shortly afterwards, when our first leaflets appeared bearing the symbol, I recall a veteran of earlier campaigns complaining to me that we must have been out of our minds when we adopted it; it had no meaning, he said, and it would never catch on.
>
> (p. 32)

Indeed, for the most part, the image is not aesthetically pleasant, neither metaphorical nor mythopoetic in nature, and yet, in the ND graphic's 65th year, it continues to root itself within the fertile ground of the collective and continue its rhizomatous peace-full work. It is curious, from a depth psychological perspective, that this specific image initially appealed to and eventually captured the attention of the collective psyche, and that today it still symbolizes

DOI: 10.4324/b23325-4

Figure 3.1 Peace Symbol. Credit: Matthew C. Clonch.

and represents the broad spectrum of issues found under the banner of peace.

Britain's Own Little Secret Leads to the Era of Mass Protests

As firm allies in the war, a small and select group of scientists and politicians from both the U.S. and Great Britain were involved in the maturation and realization of the Manhattan Project (MED) through acts of sharing information, reconnaissance, and resources. Soon after Einstein warned President Roosevelt in 1939 about the possibility of Germany working toward a nuclear weapons program, Roosevelt disclosed the matter to Great Britain's Prime Minister Winston Churchill, and it was jointly decided, for myriad reasons, that the U.S. should take lead responsibility for developing the MED (Kelly, 2007). At the time, both countries easily agreed that Great Britain's proximity to the European theater warfront—accompanied by the fear of possible detection or destruction of MED efforts and facilities—was significant reason enough for the U.S. to be tapped as host for the MED (Kelly, 2007; Dahl, 1999; Wendt & Geddes, 1945).

It became clear that if the project were to flourish and remain top secret, they would need geographical distance from possible bombings from the Axis Powers' air force as well as the geographical advantage to thwart espionage efforts from neighboring countries. The Atlantic Ocean provided that advantage to the U.S., along with its extensive tracts of land with little to no commercial or residential development, eventually allowing the MED to operate its "secret cities" in complete privacy (Kelly, 2007). Geographical distance coupled with extreme secrecy measures ensured that the U.S. could effectively maintain confidentiality of the MED until it surprise-bombed Japan and intentionally exposed its operation worldwide. Following WWII, as the collective struggled to understand the ramifications and consequences of what it meant to be ushered into the nuclear age, and though there were both initial and enduring dissents and critiques of the U.S.'s use of nuclear weapons technologies against a civilian populace (Hasegawa, 2007; Morley, 2007), the nuclear arms race commenced two years later, in 1947, when the Cold War between the world's two superpowers—the U.S. and the Soviet Union—began.

Not long after Hiroshima and Nagasaki's destruction, information leaked out about Britain's copiously supportive involvement in the MED, which increased Britain's citizen concerns about the eventual stockpiling of nuclear weapons within Britain's borders. Although Britain had knowledge of and access to nuclear weapons intelligence, Britain did not actually pursue nuclear weapons production until after the Soviet Union detonated their first atomic weapon in 1949 (Schweber, 2000; Kelly, 2007). Thus, in the years subsequent to 1950, several small-scale efforts to nonviolently protest nuclear armaments surfaced in Britain. Aldermaston, a village located approximately 52 miles from London, was repeatedly chosen as the site for the protests due to its proximity to the Atomic Weapons Establishment (AWE) factory—Great Britain's 1950 nuclear deterrence response to the neonate Cold War—which resides one mile south of the village and continues, still today, to house the design and manufacture of nuclear warheads.

In 1954, the same year as *Gojira*'s evocative movie debut in Japan, Britain began pursuing a more destructive and powerful hydrogen bomb program, and according to Kolsbun (2008), the Christmas Island hydrogen bomb tests provoked British citizens' concerns for the reason that its blast—a 1,000 times more powerful than the uranium or plutonium atomic bombs of 1945—could propel radioactive debris into the upper atmosphere, which had the potential to settle back down to earth "thousands of miles from the site of the original explosion. There it could contaminate food, be absorbed into the bones of children and adults, and eventually cause cancer" (pp. 28–29). Responding to this potential life-threatening hazard, the desire on the part of activists to go beyond acute protests materialized, but attempts to create a longer and more sustainable ND campaign met with limited success and quickly fizzled (Duff, 1971, p. 118).

Peggy Duff, organizing and general secretary for the CND between the years of 1958 and 1965, corroborates in her memoir, *Left, Left, Left* (1971), that 1957 became a year when Britain's public outcry against nuclear weapons "suddenly zoomed up" (p. 118). Randle (1986) corroborates that these Christmas Island tests "aroused a great deal of public interest and support and coincided with a new mood in Britain, following the Suez aggression of the previous year and the Soviet invasion of Hungary" (p. 31). Of the hydrogen bomb tests in the Pacific, Duff notes they not only were "the first stimulus" to radically stir public affect, but were also "a constant and very present reminder of the menace of nuclear weapons, affecting especially the health of children, and of babies yet unborn.... . The Christmas Island tests, because they were British tests, at least roused opinion in Britain" (p. 118). Thus, if we chronologically track Britain's cultural actions and responses to the presence of nuclear weapons, it seems to have taken 12 years from the 1945 U.S. atomic bomb detonations for *kairos*, or the precise occasion in time when an individual or a collective gives "their attention to one possibility rather than another," allowing a change to "the direction of their intentions and dreams" (May, 1991, p. 92), to emerge in Great Britain in favor of pacifist groups.

When the CND officially and publicly debuted in February 1958, it was their decision to hold a four-day mass march from London to Aldermaston over Easter weekend in 1958 that sparked and rallied activists. For it was the nearly synchronous formation of the DAC and the CND just three months apart that finally provided a way for radical pacifists to use the techniques of nonviolent action, to address larger audiences, exchange ideas with other radicals, join together to confront and oppose the state, and establish radical pacifism as a "significant tendency in the emerging New Left" (Ostergaard, 1986, p. 154). The more demure CND aspired to

> change public opinion and the policies of the political parties through the usual democratic channels... . [It was] not in favour of civil disobedience or sabotage so long as reasonable

opportunities continue to exist for bringing democratic pressure on Parliament.

(Canon John Collins, as quoted in Duff, 1971, p. 168)

This less radical approach appealed to CND's moderate, suburban, and largely middle-class base (Kolsbun, 2008, p. 32). With this wide scope of support, the CND almost immediately outshined and nearly appropriated the smaller and more severe DAC, but was able to work closely with the DAC to become sister organizations "working for the same ends, by different methods, mostly with the same troops, maintaining friendly relations" (Duff, 1971, p. 166).

When the ad hoc march committee first came together toward the end of February 1958 to plan hurriedly for the impending march, a sympathetic professional artist and a long-time follower of the British nuclear problematic, Gerald Holtom, walked into the office (Randle, 1986; Miles, 2008). Holtom, a conscientious objector during WWII (Campaign for Nuclear Disarmament, n.d.a), recently attended DAC and CND public meetings, felt invigorated and inspired by what he experienced in those public spaces, and joined the DAC (Kolsbun, 2008; Miles, 2008). He now approached the organizing committee to see if they could use his help; he had been thinking very seriously about the visual aesthetics necessary to make a mass campaign attractive, effective, and efficient; not only to appeal to the British public, but to also appeal to the British press and any potential media coverage (Miles, 2008). Holtom's ideas for a simple visual aid that could be easily recognized from far distances and could also be reproduced rather quickly and by anyone were appealing to the ad hoc committee members who were already feeling the strain of what Randle (1986) describes as

> alternating feelings of exhilaration and panic. Exhilaration because support for the march grew beyond our wildest imaginings; panic because… .., it seemed impossible to imagine how our tiny group could cope with the organizational problems that this degree of support had thrown up.
>
> (p. 32)

By his own volition, Holtom offered to organize and supervise the entire visual design process of the march, and unsurprisingly, the overwhelmed committee eagerly allowed him to take the lead in this endeavor (Kolsbun, 2008; Miles, 2008).

"A Human Being in Despair"

As Gerald Holtom (1961) later described the historical event in his *Peace News* article "The ND Symbol," the ND image was designed on February 21, 1958 and was "adopted immediately by the DAC who initiated and organized the First Aldermaston March at Easter that year" (p. 6) (see Figure 3.2). The article continues with Holtom's recollection of the very moments of the ND image's origination:

> First thoughts on the need for a symbol (February 19, 1958) flowed from the obvious practical difficulty of making [a] large number [of] "fore and aft" long banners with the words Unilateral Nuclear Disarmament—words which are too long for the majority of people to read or understand. The first mark on the paper was a white circle upon a black square. This was

Figure 3.2 One of Holtom's Many ND Sketches (1958). Original sketch copyright Commonweal Collection, University of Bradford, Bradford, England.

followed by various versions of Christian crosses drawn within the white "sphere" on a black background and these in turn gave way to the final ND form. All these versions of symbols were displayed on cards 20 inches square at the inaugural meeting of the London CND and received no comment other than a dislike for those showing the cross motif. Realisation dawned that the Crusaders had used the Cross in Malta, the Victoria Cross in Britain, the Iron Cross in Germany and the Croix de Guerre in France, together with the awful fact that the Christian Cross in 1958 was associated in the public mind throughout the world with the manufacture, testing and blessing of A and H-bombs.

From that moment the validity of the Symbol as a gesture of human despair became clear, and a waterproof "lollypop" was made forthwith and planted outside in the garden for testing in bad weather.
   The central motif: A human being in despair.
   A circle: The world.
   The background: Eternity.
   That was the meaning of the ND sign carried on the Aldermaston March as a [practical step towards unilateral disarmament and world disarmament, without] which life would cease. [The words in brackets are Holtom's, but were printed in erroneous order in *Peace News*. I rearranged them to make the most syntactical and grammatical sense.]

(p. 6)

The "lollypop" to which he refers is the initial design of the march's standard, a large squared or circular ND image mounted atop a lightweight piece of wood, or lath, which resembled the childhood candy treat and became the affectionate nickname for the standards used by the predominately young marchers (see Figures 3.3 and 3.4).
   In 1973, Holtom wrote to his friend Hugh Brock, editor of *Peace News*, a more personal retelling of February 21, 1958, the day he actually designed the symbol. Holtom describes himself as feeling despondent about the political and nuclear climate he and his family found themselves in:

Symbol 59

Figure 3.3 Marcher with CND Lollypop. Original photograph copyright Campaign for Nuclear Disarmament, London, England. With Permission: cnduk.org

> I was in despair. Deep despair. I drew myself: the representative of an individual in despair, with hands palm outstretched outwards and downwards in the manner of Goya's peasant before the firing squad. I formalised the drawing into a line and put circle around it.... it was ridiculous at first and such a puny thing.
> (As quoted in Miles, 2008, pp. 78–80)

Although the painting Holtom refers to in the Hugh Brock letter actually shows a man with his arms outstretched upwards in surrender (see Figure 3.5), Miles (2008) contends that Holtom may have also been influenced by another one of Goya's images from his *Disasters of War* series (see Figure 3.6). The *Disasters of War* woodcut series are widely understood in art historian circles to be visual protests against several violent uprisings in 1808 Spain, and

60 *Symbol*

Figure 3.4 First Aldermaston March Passing Through London, 1958. Original photograph copyright Campaign for Nuclear Disarmament, London, England. With Permission: cnduk.org

Goya's title and image, *Gloomy Premonitions of What Must Come to Pass*, is apropos for Holtom's essential, yet unassuming, role in the mushrooming ND movement—he belongs to the long legacy and lineage of visual artists who use their skills to publicly protest ideological state apparatuses.

On Easter weekend April 4–7, 1958, 5,000 British citizens gathered in London's Trafalgar Square to become part of the iconoclastic and communal call to direct action against nuclear weapons, to hear domestic and international speakers rally for Unilateral Nuclear Disarmament (UND), and, perhaps even more importantly (although less likely salient to the individual marcher), to commit themselves to the principles of nonviolent protest and resistance in solidarity with the CND's policy and guidelines (Kolsbun, 2008; Miles, 2008). By the time the march arrived in the village of Aldermaston on Easter Monday three days later, thousands of people had either walked part, or all, of the march

Figure 3.5 Third of May 1808 (*El Tres de Mayo*) (1814). Oil on canvas, 266 × 345 cm (105 × 136 in). Museo del Prado, Madrid. Reproduced from Wikimedia Commons: This work is in the public domain in its country of origin and other countries and areas where the copyright term is the author's life plus 100 years or fewer. Published anywhere (or registered with the U.S. Copyright Office) before 1927 and public domain in the U.S.

route while carrying 500 of Holtom's "lollypops" and a host of banners (see Figure 3.4) (Campaign for Nuclear Disarmament, n.d.a). The CND organization, on their webpage "The History of CND," states that the first Aldermaston march

> attracted a good deal of attention and the CND symbol appeared everywhere. From the outset people from all sections of society got involved. There were scientists, more aware than anyone else of the full extent of the dangers which nuclear weapons represented, along with religious leaders such as Canon John Collins of St. Paul's Cathedral, concerned to resist the moral evil which nuclear weapons represented. The Society of

62 *Symbol*

Figure 3.6 Plate 1: Sad Presentiments of What Must Come to Pass (*Tristes presentimientos de lo que ha de acontecer*) from the Disasters of War Series (*Los Desatres de la Guerra*) (1810s). Reproduced from Wikimedia Commons: This work is in the public domain in its country of origin and other countries and areas where the copyright term is the author's life plus 100 years or fewer. Published anywhere (or registered with the U.S. Copyright Office) before 1927 and public domain in the U.S.

Friends (Quakers) was very supportive, as well as a wide range of academics, journalists, writers, actors and musicians. Labour Party members and trade unionists were overwhelmingly sympathetic. (Campaign for Nuclear Disarmament, n.d.b.)

Norman Moss printed a further narrative of the historic Aldermaston march in the April 17, 1965 edition of the *Saturday Review*:

By the end of the march on Easter Monday, 10,000 people were standing in a wet and chilly field opposite the barbed wire perimeter of Aldermaston's plant to hear the speeches. Something new had happened...... The Ban the Bomb movement in Britain was a unique phenomenon and an important one. There has been nothing quite like it anywhere else in the world. It is a special byproduct of the British circumstances and the British conscience.

(As quoted in Kolsbun, 2008, p. 41)

The uniqueness of the CND and its marches lies in its early years, when, as Duff (1971) explains in her account, it was able to unite under its symbol "a very wide spectrum of people and organizations with widely differing approaches in terms of politics, morals, religion and methods of working" (p. 208). In these mass demonstrations, marchers became anonymous, faceless, and homeless, the "big names" mixing in and merging seamlessly into "the march" (p. 132). For the duration of a few days, the march became a community that required "no vows," only a willingness to "step off the pavement and join" (p. 132). She makes it clear that the march was not a "nice, cosy [sic] minority movement," or a "collection of well-meaning people seeking limited reforms like capital punishment or abortion reform," but rather like a "stage army of the good grown rather larger than usual. [The marchers] wanted a revolution... ." (p. 143). Also, given Norman Moss' assessment of the event's exceptionality, it is fascinating to note that the small pantheon of symbols already heavily in use by different peace groups of the mid-20th century—Picasso's white dove, the Japanese white (origami paper) crane, the olive branch, and rainbow—were not required or in use over the four days of the London to Aldermaston March. Instead, it was Holtom's brand new "puny thing" that was chosen to visually represent the new energy, affect, and conscience of the British ND movement.

To Be or Not to Be?

Before engaging in a depth psychological analysis of the image, it is essential to first delineate the psychological import of differing visual devices such as *symbol*, *image*, *sign*, *icon*, *emblem*, *logo*, *brand-image*, and *insignia*, as some may question whether the ND image could be considered a symbol from a psychological perspective. To determine how the ND image functions and labors in the different social and liberation movements associated with it, determination from which visual device the ND image draws its energy is needed. This is an important consideration, and in the book thus far I have intentionally referred to the ND graphic as an *image*, not a *symbol*, *sign*, or other visual device, so as not to produce a hasty assumption or conclusion for the reader.

The *Oxford English Dictionary* (*OED*) (online version January 2023) offers the following definitions for selected terms and a review of the applicability of these terms for the ND image is provided afterwards:

Image, n.: Such an imitation delineated, painted, executed in relief, stamped, or otherwise produced on a surface; a likeness, portrait, picture, carving, or the like.

(Image, n.d.)

Sign, n.: 1. An action, mark, notice, etc., conveying information or instructions, and related senses. 2. A distinctive emblem or badge borne on a banner, shield, etc., serving to make known the identity or allegiance of its bearer or followers; such an emblem worn as part of a person's livery or uniform, or as an indication of status. Also occasionally: a distinctive item used in the same way.

(Sign, n.d.)

Icon, n.: A person or thing regarded as a representative symbol, esp. of a culture or movement; a person, institution, etc., considered worthy of admiration or respect. Frequently with modifying word.

(Icon, n.d.)

Emblem, n.: A picture of an object (or the object itself) serving as a symbolical representation of an abstract quality, an action, state of things, class of persons, etc.

(Emblem, n.d.)

Logo, n.: A symbol, as found in road-signs, advertising, &c., designed to represent in simple graphic form an object, concept, or attitude.

(Logo, n.d.)

Brand-image, n: The impression of a product in the minds of potential users or consumers; also *transferred* and *figurative.*, the general or popular conception of some person or thing.

(Brand-image, n.d.)

Insignia, n.: Badges or distinguishing marks of office or honour; emblems of a nation, person, etc.

(Insignia, n.d.)

Symbol, n.: Something that stands for, represents, or denotes something else (not by exact resemblance, but by vague suggestion, or by some accidental or conventional relation); *esp.* a material object representing or taken to represent something immaterial or abstract, as a being, idea, quality, or condition; a representative or typical figure, sign, or token; *occasionally* a type (of some quality).

(Symbol, n.d.)

With respect to the ND graphic, image is, in part, an accurate descriptor. The graphic is often reproduced on myriad surfaces and textiles or graffitied in public spaces. However, it does not serve as an imitation of the concept of peace, nor is it created in the "likeness" of peace, and therefore does not fully embody the *image* definition. When Holtom describes the graphic as "the composite basic form of semaphore signal for the letters N and D" (June 2, 1961, p. 6), he is indicating that the graphic, at one register, functions effectively as a *sign* as the semaphore letters technically take the place of the words for **N**uclear **D**isarmament (flag semaphore is a maritime system of signaling letters using two flags, one held in each hand) (see Figure 3.7). However, as we have already noted and will discuss further in Part IV, it does not take long before the graphic's myopic predisposition to represent the issue of ND extends considerably and is able to integrate additional social issues. When this happens, the graphic outworks the parameters set forth by the definition of *sign*. *Icon* possibly works if it is applied loosely, but the graphic is not of a person or a thing regarded as a representative of something worthy of admiration and respect—it is not a personification of peace nor does its form suggest its meaning.

In some instances, *emblem* could be an appropriate description when the graphic is used as a distinctive badge, but again, the

66 *Symbol*

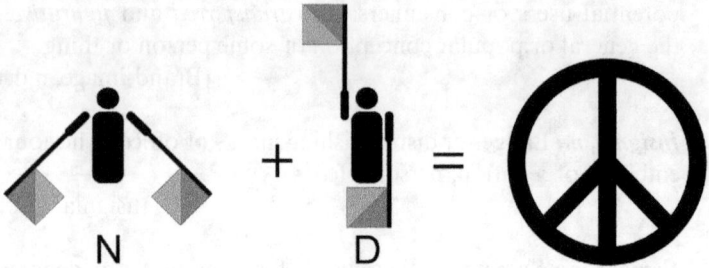

Figure 3.7 Flag Semaphore for Letters "N" and "D" and the Peace Symbol. Credit: Matthew C. Clonch.

actual graphic is not a picture of an object, or the object of "peace" itself, serving as a symbolic representation. Often, the visual device of *emblem* is employed in mythological, religious, and spiritual art, when an animal or object is painted to represent a god, goddess, or saint, or to indicate a tracing and recording of genealogy. *Logo*, on the other hand, has merit for our consideration. The ND graphic is simple, designed to represent a concept, and organizations used it heavily in their marketing and advertising strategies. In its early use, the graphic did indeed identify the ND movement and considering it to be a logo would be appropriate for that time. However, we will soon explore more closely what happens with the graphic when it crosses the Atlantic Ocean and becomes integrated in other social movements in the U.S. Thus, its explicit use as an identifying image solely for ND purposes wanes considerably and in time the *logo* foothold erodes in the visual economy. Lastly, as the ND graphic has never been copyrighted or belonged to any one group in particular (Duff, 1971), the definitions for *brand-image*, and *insignia* do not quite apply to the full circumstances of this particular graphic.

This brings us to the visual device of *symbol* as defined by the OED. In-line with this definition, the ND graphic does not exactly resemble peace, but does denote peace through a vague and conventional relation—protesters carrying the standards during marches, or passing out leaflets and bulletins, initiated with the public the psychological process of visual operant conditioning by linking and associating the graphic with the concept of UND. Likewise, as the image's mantle of associated causes and issues proliferated in the 1960s, the graphic was not only connected with survival by ND, but began to be connected with the coarse concepts "of protest, of defiance, of resistance" (Duff, 1971, p. 117), and inevitably with the more broad, abstract, and archetypal concepts of peace and justice. As a response to this ideological shift, or perhaps because of it, the ND-graphic-as-cultural-object easily slipped under or over cultural boundaries or borders, circulated about, and out of the terms selected and investigated in this chapter, best aligns with the conventional definition of *symbol*.

Symbolic Form Against Psychological Chaos

Now that we have determined that the visual device of symbol is best applied to the ND graphic, we will need to explore its depth psychological validity as a symbol. A sampling of Jung's writings (1978, 1972, 1969, 1961, 1959a) reveals the mercurial, complex, and multiplicitous nature of the symbol concept. In *Aion* (1959a), written during the 1950s and published a year after the formation of the CND, Jung postulates that symbols help to organize disconnected images that arise during chaotic psychic states. If we place the ND symbol within this consideration, it becomes one straightforward way to understand how, out of a detonated and enantiodromian radioactive psyche, the ND symbol arose to help bring together and organize disconnected post-nuclear images and visions, as well as to shunt differing intensities of individual and collective affect toward nonviolent direct action. Jung further notes in *Aion* that an individual cannot determine beforehand how she or he will interpret the presence of a pictorial symbol or what it will mean for her or him in context. To this end, the ND symbol offers a kaleidoscopic-process-of-sorts to honor the array of multivalent relationships available between the symbol and the interpreter in the meaning-making process; it initially guides the post-nuclear collective conscious to "see-through" the convoluted nuclear age; and it ultimately illuminates the reveal-and-conceal aspects of symbols.

Two years later Jung writes in his autobiography, *Memories, Dreams, Reflections* (1961), that when shadow becomes conscious and a cleavage occurs, symbols function as a means toward adjustment, or as a means for the tension of opposites to seek compensation in unity (p. 335). When the Manhattan Project became conscious in 1945 and a cleavage ensued—in the form of the nuclear age, or enantiodromia—there was not an existing symbol readily available to come forward and deeply respond to the serious predicament of a radioactive psyche. Echoing Jung's sentiment that a "symbol is an unconscious invention in answer to a conscious problematic" (Samuels, Shorter, & Plaut, 1986, p. 146), Hillman (1975) advocates that when we are able to bridge inner ideas with outer actions, we are able to see the world differently, and thus act in the world differently. Hence, if our radioactive psyche were now seeing differently in the post-Nagasaki and post-Hiroshima world, would it not create, or perhaps act, differently in terms of its unconscious invention to this peculiar conscious problematic?

Recall at the end of Part II that a series of circular images, produced in direct response to the nuclear problematic, were put forth as by-products of the enantiodromian psychological processes occurring within the cultural radioactive psyche. Although they, themselves, are a bit rudimentary, it is possible to argue that these images serve as modern mandalas for the collective. Jung (1969) states that when *mandala* images—Sanskrit for "circle" or "magic circle"—appear in a series, "they often follow chaotic, disordered states marked by conflict and anxiety. They express the idea of a refuge, of inner reconciliation and wholeness" (p. 100). This assertion makes sense for the radiation-warning images, UFOs, fallout shelter images, and others from the nuclear age that serve to produce an order for collective anxieties, affect, and sense of safety. Certainly, it is these attributes that allow us to loosely interpret their form and design as mandalas. Yet, within this postnuclear collection of self-contained images, the ND symbol sets itself apart.

For if we look deeply at the ND symbol, we see that it is a circle with a vertical diameter that effectively splits the circle into two equal halves; and if using Jungian semiotics, the circle can be understood as holding the tension of opposites. The vertical diameter forks half way down and split the halves into further parts, effectively creating a quaternity where the top two parts are not equal in size to the bottom two parts. The circle provides a container for the fragmentation, the splitting, and the disintegration of the space within. Although an oddity in the pantheon of peace symbols, Holtom's "human being in despair" emerged spontaneously and functions as a symbolic lacunar bridge: it depicts a denuded and cryptic human figure offering the unique opportunity to reflect and mirror the interpreter's literal self, figurative self, and the interpreter's affect (e.g., despair, anxiety, survival). More importantly, however, whatever meaning is made between the symbol and the interpreter, it is safely contained within the womb of Holtom's circle.

If we accept that the ND symbol was first created as an individual mandala, before the collective took it up, it is easy to imagine that Holtom wanted to express his "inner or outer experience of the world, or at least [his] essential point of reference" (Jung, 1969, p. 5) through his design and technique. Holtom's writings and interviews on the subject suggest that his design represents this struggle to expression and his "human being in despair" is a representation of the *self*, which Jung (1969) notes is

> in contradistinction to the *ego*, which is the only point of reference for consciousness, whereas the self comprises the totality of the psyche altogether, i.e., conscious *and* unconscious. It is therefore not unusual for individual mandalas to display a division into a light and dark half, together with their typical symbols.
>
> (p. 5)

If we look back at Figure 3.2, an early sketch of the ND symbol by Holtom, we see that a black square, which he deemed to represent eternity, encases a white circle that represents the world. In some journalistic interviews (Tims, 1959) he suggests that the choice of colors is to demonstrate good triumphing over evil. Of course, using the language of white = good and black = evil aligns with imperialistic and oppressive rhetoric at the very minimum, *and*, in our depth psychological analysis, this language helps us to understand his color choices in terms of conscious and unconscious contents. Adding another layer of analysis likewise suggests that when a psychological element is outside the protective circle, instead of inside, it "affords protection against extreme opposites; that is, the sharpness of the conflict is not yet realized or else it is felt intolerable. The protective circle then guards against possible disruption due to the tension of the opposites" (Jung, 1969,

p. 83). In our case, the black square—which we have noted as the unconscious—is outside of and looms over, engulfs, the white circle of protected consciousness. Extreme opposites? Sharp conflict not fully realized? Feeling intolerable? Tension of opposites? Undeniably, all of these phrases accurately describe radioactive psyche's turmoil in the nuclear age and we see them manifested in Holtom's original squaring-of-the-circle ND design.

If we also appreciate the ND symbol as a uniting symbol, or mandala, with a circle that encloses a quaternion, its emergence in 1958 is in-line with Jung's belief that circle and quaternity symbolism appear as a compensating principle of order that arises from the "collision between the conscious and the unconscious and from the confusion which this causes… . this confusion takes the form of restlessness and disorientation" (1959a, p. 194). When the incredible secrecy measures that kept the Manhattan Project in the country's psychological shadow were revealed to the collective, a nuclear-filled confusion unquestionably befuddled the collective into years of restlessness and disorientation. We collectively struggled with the consequences of a newly militarized science and its heinous outcomes, which occurred contemporaneously with nuclear paranoia and unspecified diffuse affect about our own survival; and as one result, the era of science fiction movies and novels—places where new solutions to nuclear and technology problems could be imagined and tried out without consequence—emerged and successfully proliferated. As we discussed in Part II, from the underground fallout shelters signs below to the UFOs in the skies above, circular imagery ubiquitously appeared in visual culture in response to the novel psycho-climate of the nuclear age.

Again, what is especially powerful about the ND symbol's design is that it possesses a tetradic design within a circle. The archetypal 4, which has myriad interpretations across the disciplines of thought and religious traditions, denotes from a psychoanalytic lens a "coming to consciousness of an unconscious content" and as such, frequently occurs is cosmogenic myths (Jung, 1969, pp. 37–38). As we have discussed, the MED and the CND contribute to Western eschatological (apocalypse) and cosmogenic (rebirth) myth-making as a means for the collective to deal with potent unconscious content becoming conscious (e.g., we are now capable of world-wide immolation, when previously this function was reserved only for god/s). As circle and quaternity symbols tend to "depict the union of warring opposites as already accomplished, and thus ease[ing] the way to a healthier and quieter state" (pp. 194–195), the ND circle and quaternity embody the future oriented intention of the CND—to bring to pass a world free of the threat of nuclear annihilation and a healthier and quieter world for future generations. In this same spirit, Jung notes that mandalas are "birthplaces, vessels of birth in the most literal sense" (1954/1959b, p. 130) where possibilities and promise can thrive. For the Plutonian-like origins of the CND and its sister organizations, these archetypal and mythological underpinnings provide a powerful impetus for their quest to dismantle and overturn the deeply entrenched status quo.

The design of the ND symbol is not the only principal consideration for our inquiry; the timing of its emergence is as well. As we have already mentioned, in a cursory comparative analysis of historical Western peace symbols, the ND symbol is a tenderfoot, emerging into the visual cultural economy a little over 65 years ago, whereas peace symbols such as the white dove, the olive branch, or rainbow have their origins based in centuries old Judeo-Christian or Eurocentric traditions. These traditional peace symbols represent the natural world and herald distinct qualities of peace—qualities that we will not explicate further here, yet refer the interested reader to Rosenthal's (1994) *How on Earth Does an Olive Branch Mean Peace?*, Von Franz's (1980) *Alchemy: An Introduction to the Symbolism and the Psychology*, and Hillman's (1981) *Silver and the White Earth Part II*. However, the ND symbol, which purports a Eurocentric genesis, also has an anthropogenic origin and responds to an anthropogenic problematic: the threat of nuclear annihilation. With these circumstances in mind, a never-seen-before symbol might have very well needed to emerge in order to deal with the never-experienced-before nuclear peril, a peril to the collective psyche that the traditional symbols of peace—the white dove, the olive branch, and the rainbow—could not contain within their time-honored and earth-bound symbolic roles.

To explore this position further, let us compare the ND symbol to the Pax Cultural symbol. Interestingly, the Pax Cultura symbol (Figure 3.8) is another anthropogenic circular symbol, but one that traces its lineage back to Stone Age amulets (Roerich Pact and Banner of Peace Through Culture, n.d.). According to the document, "Roerich Pact and Banner of Peace Through Culture",

72 *Symbol*

Figure 3.8 Pax Cultura Symbol. Credit: Matthew C. Clonch.

the symbol experienced an international renaissance during the 1920s and 1930s as "The Banner of Peace" in connection with the Roerich Pact movement that strived to preserve and protect cultural heritages, artifacts, activities, and institutions from the "ravages of war and neglect." The symbol, understood in ancient times to represent a "deep and sophisticated understanding of the triune nature of existence," was employed by the Roerich Pact[1] movement to declare its users independent of combatant forces and to labor for the value of neutrality. For the purposes of the movement, which acquired the nickname "The Red Cross of Culture," the symbol was overlaid with its current meaning of "totality of culture, with the three dots being Art, Science, and Religion, three of the most embracing of human cultural activities"; whereas the circle represents "the eternity of time, encompassing the past, present, and future." Despite its rich history and longevity, the symbol's design does not inherently respond to the psychic fragmentation, splitting, and disintegration of the radioactive nuclear psyche with its three solid and self-contained circles that are able to maintain their psychic presence without their larger enclosure or boundary. Furthermore, the value for which Pax Cultura advocates—neutrality—does not befit the values of the ND movement. As such, the symbol's material design occupies an undervalued status in peace-full symbolic currency and cultural capital.

Conversely, the "fork" of the ND symbol responded to radioactive psyche, and continues to do so, but it does not translate its psychic presence to the interpreter unless it is enclosed within the safe container of the larger circle and becomes a single "forked circle" unit. This slight difference in the psychological import of the symbol's design helps us to better understand the ND symbol's relevance and prominence: Even though it began as an ad hoc and everyday image, it combined in the meaning-making process with the strong archetypal valences of survival, peace, and justice, allowing it to become loosened within a few years span "from its connections with other images with which it previously shared a context" and become "connected to a new context: one that is defined by the power and structure of the archetype" (Van Eenwyk, 1997, pp. 101–102). In our case study, the ND symbol labored relentlessly for UND politics alongside images of radiation signs, Polaris submarines, and the War Resisters League's broken rifle logo and yet within a few years' time it alone surpassed the symbolic ranks of the white dove, the olive branch, and the rainbow of peace and justice. All of these reflections provide additional support for asking the questions, "how come the ND graphic now means peace?" And, "how did it become relevant world-wide?"

Something Dynamic Happened

As already noted, the ND symbol was not intended to be seen or serve any purpose beyond the Aldermaston to London march of April 1958, and yet, something dynamic happened in the interaction between the image and the surround of that four-day march. The ND symbol, from its onset, was placed in a domain beyond what other traditional peace symbols at the time were—the domains of highly kinetic, widely advertised, long-range and long-term myopic mass protests. The symbol was always utilized to represent a specific condition or request, such as "action is happening right here in the present moment, come join us" or "action is needed in the near future, will you join us?" Dissimilar to the familiar rainbow or olive branch, which routinely and passively suggests a broad, mostly nebulous *value* of peace, the ND symbol, in its nascent incarnation, always meant *action* toward UND. This essential characteristic, which stems from its participation in the meaning-making of the mass protest marches and rallies, is a major component that sets the symbol apart from others of its kind. The ND symbol became invested with a unique meaning when it was first seen in the context of the CND's novel en masse walking marches and rallies, occasions of great importance for public solidarity and resistance in Britain. Due to the symbol's principal role of marshalling the historic marches, it is credited as necessary, possibly even sacred, to the campaign's success (Kolsbun, 2008; Miles, 2008; Duff, 1971). While suggesting that the symbol is *sacred* to the secular and political social movement conceivably teeters on hyperbole, the notion of an ecclesiastical purpose and framework for the march does not. DAC members intentionally selected to schedule the march on holy Easter weekend as it is the quintessential time of year when the Christian calendar (chronos) intersects with the core Christian myth of death and rebirth (kairos), or what Ulansey (2000) suggests is "an almost universal symbolic representation of the experience of transformation" (p. 224).

Planning an event for Easter weekend—with the intention of using it as a foundational container for a transformative experience—was a well-known strategy of the nonviolent ND movement. A "Let's Walk for Peace" march bulletin from the U.S.-based Committee for Nonviolent Action (CNVA) offers a typical example of this strategy and reads, "We expect to arrive there on Easter Sunday to symbolize our hope for a new and better world" (Let's Walk for Peace, n.d.). The abundant symbolism of the Easter/Aldermaston march was also not lost on Gerald Holtom—he capitalized on the fortuitous occasion and is quoted in Kolsbun (2008) as stating:

> This was an Easter March: the ancient Spring Solstice Festival to which Christianity had attached the Celebration of the crucifixion and the resurrection ceremony. From Winter to Spring, from Death to Life. It was my intention to use the black and white symbols on Friday and Saturday and change to green on Sunday and Monday as a token gesture and prelude to a more dramatic revolutionary action, which I had planned to develop in years to come.
>
> The leader [of the march] was the pace-maker and he was followed by a large banner which simply proclaimed "March from London to Aldermaston" with lettering that passing drivers could see 400 yards away and read at 150 yards. The UND Symbol was in gold leaf and at the top corners for luminous reflection of car headlights at night.... . I made pockets in the main banners so that they would take a bunch

of spring flowers on Easter Sunday and Monday. Few people noticed them and of those who did, most wept... . . I intended the lollypops to be stuck into the ground on their wood laths at stopping places so that they would appear like a Field of Remembrance in which a great family picnic was taking place. It never quite happened like that, but it might do yet.

(p. 36)

Duff (1971) recalls her experiencing of the "stark and funereal" colors of white on black or black on white as "part of the symbolism," and carrying the "daffodils [was] a symbol of life and the spring" (p. 115). Indeed, half of the 500 lollypops carried on the 1958 Aldermaston march were black on white, while the other half were white on green and that "just as the church's liturgical colors change over Easter, so the colours were to change" (Campaign for Nuclear Disarmament, n.d.a). And, although the lollypops did not take on the Field of Remembrance configuration that Holtom hoped for, the symbol effectively and tirelessly continued to work and broadcast the presence of the campaign as marchers propped them on trees, on sides of building, or leaned on them as they, themselves, stopped and rested.

In her June 1959 article, "ND and the Artist," Margaret Tims perceptively reports what she views as the combined strengths of the ND "lollypop" symbol and the CND, a mere 14 months after the first Aldermaston march debuted:

Too often mass campaigns have fallen into the hands of politicians and propagandists who, however dedicated, are out of touch with the basic realities; who lack also the magic spark that can ignite a manifesto and set off a chain reaction through the national consciousness.

The first Aldermaston march had this kind of magic; so had its symbol, the semaphore ND "lollypop," which caught the public imagination with extraordinary effect. Artists deal in symbols more than most people, and perhaps that is why they support the campaign, not as an *alternative* to pacifism, but as being the most *appropriate* response to the present situation. As the H-bomb is the symbol of all the forces of destruction, so ND has become the symbol of all the countering forces of creation: life against death, love against hate, form against chaos.

A convenient simplification, maybe: but a necessary one, if the meaning of life is to be restored to the ordinary bewildered human being... .

Gerald Holtom's "shorthand" symbol has the double advantage of providing identity for the marcher and easy recognition for the onlooker. Its deeper meaning he explains as symbolizing "the little man in despair," and, by the white emblem on a black ground, the triumph of good over evil... .

What's wrong with the Cross as a symbol, it may be wondered? But the sad fact is that the meaning of the Cross has been so overlaid by Church and State that it is *not* easily perceived... . It is therefore necessary to invent new symbols to explain the old truths. ... .

It is here that the artist comes into his own, and here that he has an opportunity to break through the prison of his own consciousness and become one with his fellows. Gerald Holtom has described it as "the struggle for expression through technique," and he feels that the Aldermaston marches did achieve a synthesis of this kind.

(p. 2)

In this *Peace News* article, Tims suggests that the enigmatic energy around the Aldermaston march and the ND symbol is connected, in some way, with their ability to bring together, or at least respond to, opposing ideals: life against death, rebirth against apocalypse, love against hate, peace against war, creation against destruction, form against chaos, community against individualism, H-Bomb against ND movement, government against citizen populace, and the triumph of good over evil. Tims is pointing toward the ND symbol, suggesting that it is an image that amalgamates opposites into a symbolic union, that its essence is able to generate and to direct the energies and affect of the campaigners for a particular time and place and, together with all the actors in the network, create an open-yet-bounded meaning-full relationship—in the context of nonviolent direct action—between the campaigners and the symbol, and the marchers and the onlookers. Although her observations are, again, filled with the bipolarity that often finds itself in discourses of the West, and in peace-related discourses in particular, she provides a solid and valid insight into how the symbol functioned in the campaign.

In the 65 years since nuclear energy was militarized and the horrific effects of nuclear detonation were experienced in Hiroshima and Nagasaki, no country has set off a nuclear warhead on another country. Yet, with the loom and menace of nuclear destruction possibilities proliferating as additional countries choose to become nuclear states, and with catastrophic natural events endangering the structures and production plants that supply nuclear energy, we continue to live in a loaded nuclear age. For instance, on March 11, 2011 a tsunami crashed ashore the coast of Japan and caused such significant damage to one of its nuclear energy plants that Japanese personnel worked furiously for days and weeks on end to prevent another Chernobyl (1986) or Three Mile Island (1979) nuclear disaster from occurring. Since then, additional nuclear incidents of varying degrees have been recorded, including in the U.S. and UK. Over half a century later, it seems radioactive psyche is still a viable and relevant descriptor of the psychological milieu now shared across intergenerational populations of the world.

Thus, our purpose in deeply studying the ND symbol, which was born out of the same predicament of persistent nuclear peril in which we find ourselves today, is not an exercise in the utilization of a reductionistic framework, but a means, as Jung describes it, to "attribute hermeneutic significance to [the symbol] consistent with its value and meaning" (as quoted in Van Eenwyk, 1997, p. 104). The challenge in working with symbols, however, is that they, more or less, attempt to elucidate something that is "still entirely unknown or still in the process of formation" (Van Eenwyk, 1997, p. 104). And in the case of the ND symbol's emergence, we remain in the early stages of understanding the consequences of our Promethean act—to which the symbol responds. In *Mandala Symbolism* (1969), Jung suggests that lingering over images "for a long time" (p. 65) helps to integrate unconscious contents into consciousness through a psychic evolution that anticipates future developments:

> These psychic evolutions do not as a rule keep pace with the tempo of intellectual developments. Indeed, their very first goal is to bring a consciousness that has hurried too far ahead into contact again with the unconscious background with which it should be connected. The tempo of development of consciousness through science and technology was too rapid and left the

unconscious, which could no longer keep up with it, far behind, thereby forcing it into a defensive position which expresses itself in a universal will to destruction.

(p. 65)

This observation offers some understanding into why a 13-year delay exists from when the world first learned in 1945 about its scientific nuclear annihilation intelligence to 1958 when a symbol was created that would effectively engage with a radioactive collective to bring consciousness to nonviolent direct action as a means to survive, protest, defy, and resist. Shortly after its debut, the ND symbol became a wide-reaching phenomenon in the global visual economy, and in our time, the image ultimately indicates a broad notion of peace and justice whenever and wherever it is used politically, and as such, it is the case study's center point of inquiry.

Note

1 Franklin Roosevelt signed the international Roerich Pact treaty along with all members of the Pan-American Union on April 15, 1935. Additional countries later signed it and it claims Albert Einstein as one of its preeminent endorsers. (Roerich Pact and Banner of Peace Through Culture, n.d.)

References

Brand-image. (n.d.). In *Oxford English dictionary online*. Retrieved from www-oed-com.ezproxy.rollins.edu/view/Entry/22627

Campaign for Nuclear Disarmament, (1958, April 14). Minutes of the Meeting of the Executive Committee [Microfilm edition]. Campaign for Nuclear Disarmament Archives (Reel 132.1, w1/7). Swarthmore College Peace Collection, Swarthmore, PA.

Campaign for Nuclear Disarmament, (n.d.a). The CND symbol. Retrieved from https://cnduk.org/the-symbol/

Campaign for Nuclear Disarmament, (n.d.b.). The history of CND. Retrieved from https://cnduk.org/who/the-history-of-cnd/

Dahl, P. F. (1999). *Heavy water and the wartime race for nuclear energy*. Bristol, England: Taylor & Francis.

Duff, P. (1971). *Left, left, left: A personal account of six protest campaigns 1945–1965*. London, England: Allison & Busby.

Emblem. (n.d.). In *Oxford English dictionary online*. Retrieved from www-oed-com.ezproxy.rollins.edu/view/Entry/60880

Hasegawa, T. (2007). Massive pain, suffering, and horror. In C. Kelly (Ed.), *The Manhattan Project: The birth of the atomic bomb in the words of its creators, eyewitnesses, and historians*. (pp. 330–332). New York, NY: Black Dog & Leventhal.
Hillman, J. (1975). *Revisioning psychology*. New York, NY: Harper and Row.
Hillman, J. (1981). Silver and the white earth (part two). *Spring: An Annual of Archetypal Psychology and Jungian Thought, 21*–66. Dallas, TX: Spring.
Holtom, G. (1961, June 2). The ND symbol. *Peace News: The International Pacifist Weekly*, p. 6.
Icon. (n.d.). In *Oxford English dictionary online*. Retrieved from www-oed-com.ezproxy.rollins.edu/view/Entry/90879
Image. (n.d.). In *Oxford English dictionary online*. Retrieved from www-oed-com.ezproxy.rollins.edu/view/Entry/91618
Insignia. (n.d.). In *Oxford English dictionary online*. Retrieved from www-oed-com.ezproxy.rollins.edu/view/Entry/96839
Jung, C. G. (1959a). *Aion*. Princeton, NJ: Princeton University Press.
Jung, C. G. (1959b). Archetypes of the collective unconscious (R. F. C. Hull, Trans.) In H. Read et al. (Series Eds.), *The collected works of C. G. Jung* (Vol. 9i, pp. 3–41). Princeton, NJ: Bollingen/Princeton University Press. (Original work published 1954)
Jung, C. G. (1961). *Memories, dreams, reflections*. New York, NY: Vintage Books.
Jung, C. G. (1969). *Mandala symbolism*. Princeton, NJ: Princeton University Press.
Jung, C. G. (1972). *Two essays on analytical psychology*. Princeton, NJ: Princeton University Press.
Jung, C. G. (1978). *Flying saucers: A modern myth of things seen in the skies*. New York, NY: MJF Books.
Kelly, C. C. (2007). *The Manhattan Project: The birth of the atomic bomb in the words of its creators, eyewitnesses, and historians*. New York, NY: Black Dog & Leventhal.
Kolsbun, K. (2008). *Peace: The biography of a symbol*. Washington, DC: National Geographic Society.
Let's walk for peace. (n.d.). Committee for Nonviolent Action Files. Swarthmore College Peace Collection.
Logo. (n.d.). In *Oxford English dictionary online*. Retrieved from www-oed-com.ezproxy.rollins.edu/view/Entry/109829
May, R. (1991). *The cry for myth*. New York, NY: Dell.
Miles, B. (2008). *Peace: 50 years of protest*. Pleasantville, NY: Reader's Digest Association.
Morley, F. (2007). The return to nothingness. In C. Kelly (Ed.), *The Manhattan Project: The birth of the atomic bomb in the words of*

its creators, eyewitnesses, and historians (pp. 399–400). New York, NY: Black Dog & Leventhal.

Ostergaard, G. (1986). Liberation and development: Gandhian and Pacifist perspectives. In G. Chester & A. Rigby (Eds.), *Articles of peace: Celebrating fifty years of Peace News* (pp. 142–168). Bridport, Dorset: Prism Press.

Randle, M. (1986). Pacifism, war resistance, and the struggle against nuclear weapons: Part I: From conscientious objection to nonviolent resistance. In G. Chester & A. Rigby (Eds.), *Articles of peace: Celebrating fifty years of Peace News* (pp. 27–36). Bridport, Dorset: Prism Press.

Roerich Pact and banner of peace through culture. (n.d.). In *Nicholas Roerich museum*. Retrieved January 7, 2023 from www.roerich.org/roerich-pact.php

Rosenthal, P. (1994, April). How on earth does an olive branch mean peace? *Peace & Change, 19* (2), 165. doi: http://dx.doi.org/10.1111/j.1468-0130.1994.tb00605.x

Samuels, A., Shorter, B., & Plaut, F. (1986). *A critical dictionary of Jungian analysis*. New York, NY: Routledge.

Schweber, S. S. (2000). *In the shadow of the bomb: Bethe, Oppenheimer, and the moral responsibility of the scientist*. Princeton, NJ: Princeton University Press.

Sign. (n.d.). In *Oxford English dictionary online*. Retrieved from www-oed-com.ezproxy.rollins.edu/view/Entry/179512

Symbol. (n.d.). In *Oxford English dictionary online*. Retrieved from www-oed-com.ezproxy.rollins.edu/view/Entry/196197

Tims, M. (1959, June 26). ND and the Artist. *Peace News: The International Pacifist Weekly*, p. 2.

Ulansey, D. (2000). Cultural transition and spiritual transformation: From Alexander the Great to cyberspace. In T. Singer (Ed.), *The vision thing: Myth, politics and psyche in the world* (pp. 213–231). New York, NY: Routledge.

Van Eenwyk, J. R. (1997). *Archetypes and strange attractors: The chaotic world of symbols*. Toronto: Inner City Books.

Von Franz, M-L. (1980). *Alchemy: An introduction to the symbolism and the psychology*. Toronto: Inner City Books.

Wendt, G., & Geddes, D. P. (Eds.). (1945). *The atomic age opens*. Cleveland, OH: World Publishing.

Part IV: Kairos
Alchemizing the Golden Shadow

During the late 1940s and 1950s, the bombings mandated that the West, and Americans in particular, confront the values and motivations of our ego persona as well as the "bottle imps" lingering in our shadow, for both persona and shadow were projected out into the international community as the ego-pleasing and welcoming persona of Lady Liberty who says, "Give me your tired, your poor, your huddled masses yearning to breathe free" (Lazarus, 1883), and the destructive shadow of Uncle Sam who clandestinely unleashes a frighteningly divine technology onto the world as a demonstration of Promethean muscle. The incalculable mass destruction at the bomb's point of impact (and for future generations in inherited irradiated physical, ecological, and psychological by-products and outgrowths), confirms for the first time in human history that we possess the intelligence and engineering prowess instantaneously and irreparably to destroy ourselves and the earth. Beforehand, this highly improbable reality unfolds in the imagination of pagan and religious eschatological mythologies through the apocalyptic visions and Armageddon actions of gods and goddesses. Thus, receiving the deep and stark confirmation in 1945 of our anthropogenic annihilatory reality requires that we understand and comprehend the scope of our human limits and powers much differently than before.

As mapped in Part II, in the years subsequent to 1945, psyche struggles to comprehend and make sense of our groundbreaking Promethean war-making capabilities, while at the same time it struggles in a parallel and more chthonic register—located in the societal margins—to come to action and protest in the form of mainstream societal resistance. From a depth psychological standpoint, the nuclear crisis marks an enantiodromian intersection

DOI: 10.4324/b23325-5

between what some would argue as the worse—harboring and living under the peril of militarized nuclear energy and weapons; and the better—encouraging large-scale collective and collaborative efforts toward transnational ethical responsibility and worldwide peace.

There's Gold in the British Shadow

In *Aion* (1959a), the text written near the end of Jung's career, he suggests the human shadow not only contains sordid or distasteful psychological qualities, but legitimate and decent psychological qualities as well:

> If it has been believed hitherto that the human shadow was the source of all evil, it can now be ascertained on closer investigation that the conscious [hu]man, that is, his [or her] shadow, does not consist only of morally reprehensible tendencies, but also displays a number of good qualities, such as normal instincts, appropriate reactions, realistic insights, creative impulses, etc.
>
> (p. 266)

Zweig and Abrams (1991), post-Jungians and editors of *Meeting the Shadow: The Hidden Power of the Dark Side of Human Nature*, carry forward Jung's intuitive perception on the essentially helpful nature of the shadow by also hinting at the potentials hidden within the shadow:

> The shadow is only negative from the point of view of consciousness; it is not—as Freud insisted—totally immoral and incompatible with our conscious personalities. Rather, it potentially contains values of the highest morality. This is particularly true, says Frey–Rohn, when there is a side hidden in the shadow personality which society values as positive, yet which is regarded by the individual as inferior.
>
> (pp. 3–4)

These excerpts from both Jung and Zweig and Abrams point toward the positive, or underdeveloped potentials buried within the shadow, but neither does much to further expand the underdocumented concept. William A. Miller (1989) notices the long-established lacuna in the literature and writes *Your Golden Shadow: Discovering and Fulfilling Your Undeveloped Self*. In both psychodynamic and psychoanalytic circles, the concept of the golden shadow is much less common than the shadow, and still, in the 30+ years since Miller published his book, his observations about the golden shadow hold true: "comparatively little has been done to 'publicize' the concretely positive elements in shadow and to encourage their discovery and use" (1989, p. 14). Whereas Miller's primary aim in inquiring into the golden shadow is to encourage its use and discovery among individuals, the collectivized concept of the golden shadow assists our analysis of the Manhattan Project as a material, yet secret, government entity laboring in the shadows of the U.S.'s psyche; in our analysis of the nuclear age as an imaginative enantiodromian process often displayed in mandala and circular imagery of the time and in the emergent literature and film genres of science-fiction and post-apocalyptic horror; and again in our analysis of the nuclear disarmament (ND) symbol's "form against chaos" effect on the Peace Movement as material, yet public, nongovernment entities laboring openly in the collective psyche of the West.

Likewise, Miller asserts that "the shadow, comprised of the persona's opposite, would be a veritable goldmine of positive traits" (p. 78), and in our study, the seeds of the Peace Movement are found within the culture's shadow. Although initially covered over, the rhizomic goldmine of traits connected to aggressive and violent impulses (which are displaced onto a patriotic and militarized persona) include differing variations of nonviolent mediation, assertions of basic human rights, a coming together of disparate groups in collaboration, and life-affirming mass resistance and action. Miller further suggests, "another source of gold in shadow manifests itself in the form of a tremendous array of positive elements that exist as equal opposites to the undesirable dimensions we possess in our conscious personality" (p. 85). Shadow manifestations therefore have a concurrent temporality with persona manifestations, which suggests they exist *not* as an effect that responds to an inherent splitting of dualities, but that the shadow and persona exist in a complex interdependent relationship.

A useful visualization of the "gold seed in the shadow" concept is found in the Chinese Taoist Yin-Yang symbol (see Figure 4.1).

Figure 4.1 Taoist Yin-Yang Symbol. Credit: Matthew C. Clonch.

From a depth psychological lens, the Yin-Yang symbol itself does not purport two bipolar opposites standing firm and hedged into ongoing tensions—as does the ND symbol. The curvilinear design that separates the left side from the right side has a very different psychological import from the ND symbol's split into a left-side/right-side circle. The Yin-Yang symbol, of Eastern origins and traditions, hosts a more fluid understanding of the tension of opposites that ebbs and flows, "creating the possibility of change" (Shepherd & Shepherd, 2002, p. 341). Within the rounded and wavy opposites we find smaller circles of the reverse color and characteristic in a philosophical nod toward the idea of interdependence. While the Newtonian paradigm, which dominates Western cultures, is primarily concerned with cause-and-effect explanations, interdependence is a different idea altogether.

In a basic straightforward definition, interdependence is the idea of self-reliance and responsibilities-to-others happening concomitantly. Cause and effect, on the other hand, are often thought of as separate and dependent entities, "with cause always preceding effect, and one cause leading to one effect" (Nhat Hanh, 1988, p. 221). Thus, if we are not careful, shadow and golden shadow can also be shuffled into this type of dualistic cause-and-effect categorization, and it becomes possible to unintentionally ignore the incredibly complex psychological web that supports the peaceful seed of Yin to be contained within the hostile heart of Yang, and the peaceful heart of Yin to contain the hostile seed of Yang.

If we, instead, understand shadow and golden shadow to be co-arising interdependent notions, then we are much better able to absorb the multiplicities, complexities, and dynamics within the

Figure 4.2 Figure Ground Illusion. Credit: Matthew C. Clonch.

waxing and waning enantiodromian continuum to which it belongs. To do this, however, requires that we eschew the perspective of linear chronology—another cause-and-effect epistemological system—in favor of working within a sometimes overlapping and sometimes confusing system of co-arising spatialities and temporalities, a concept fairly well illustrated by a simple gestalt figure-ground illusion (see Figure 4.2). The figure-ground illusion allows us to visually understand that while two (or more) object figures or perceptions are always available to the interpreter, the tendency is to immediately perceive one object figure, and then put forth cognitive effort to spatially perceive and re-orient the second object figure when it "comes forward." However, both object figures exist and occur at once since one object figure cannot and does not exist without the other. The efficacy of the illusion then becomes a matter of how and when the particular interpreter perceives the multiple object figures.

Alchemizing the Golden Shadow

To this end, if we view the post-bomb era's visual cultural products from the U.S. public imaginary, one of the many places where enantiodromian processes of the cultural psyche are on display, complete with idealized and escapist storylines, is in classic U.S. television programs such as *Leave it to Beaver (1957–1963)*, *Gunsmoke (1952–1961)*, and *The Ed Sullivan Show (1948–1971)*.

As mentioned in Part II, time and again, these programs' viewing audiences experience the episode's dénouement through socially acceptable characters—who embody traits such as pleasantness, obedience, and submissiveness—exhibiting the willingness to "get back in line" after a required meager misstep so as not to disrupt the dominant culture patriarchal power structures. If we believe that these programs reflect a partial reality or imagination of the 1950s projected cultural persona and hegemony, and if we believe that the theory of the golden shadow holds merit, then simultaneously pooling below the cultural persona are the conflicting and unacceptable societal shadow traits of anger, disobedience, and rebellion (i.e., James Dean's 1955 *Rebel Without a Cause*). For segments of the population who are not involved in activities that provide socially acceptable conduits for the release of anger, aggression, and rule-breaking, such as we see in team sports or in the military's active employ (albeit these are *highly regulated* forms of affective release), it seems that the underground formation of these undesirable traits would be particularly pertinent. Where does the unacceptable and repressed *collective* affect go and where might it accumulate? Some of it is thrust up into the skies as UFOs, some of it is absorbed down into Tokyo Bay's waters for a resurrected Gojira to wreak havoc on the mainland, some of it is burrowed into the earth in the form of doomsday prepping and fallout shelters, and some of it is simply waiting for an apropos outlet.

Although the premise of the golden shadow theory is mostly based upon an individual register, we can effectively employ it on behalf of the collective. If we imagine that strong shadow emotions of internalized collective anger, fear, anxiety, disobedience, and rebellion are being developed at once within the externalized 1950s cultural persona of pleasantness and diplomacy, then, according to the golden shadow theory, the hushed, widespread, and normalized behaviors of

> denying anger its appropriate expression, necessarily relegates to shadow the power and ability to express anger appropriately. This is truly a Golden Shadow attribute, as is the power and ability to express appropriately *any* strong feeling that has had to be repressed because of the expectations of one's subculture.
> (Miller, 1989, p. 91)

Throughout the 1950s, divergent groups in both the U.S. and Britain lay the groundwork to locate and utilize the constructive and useful potentials of the psychological dimensions of collective anger, fear, anxiety, disobedience, and rebellion. Through sensible observations, clever strategy, and utmost courage these groups re-engage the unsavory qualities quashed—by an agreeable cultural persona—into the depths of cultural shadow. They likewise creatively endeavor to reintroduce into collective consciousness, in the name of justice and equality the discarded qualities of the golden shadow. And each distinct group, along with the assistance of its shrewd leaders, harnesses the available power and ability to express their anger—and interconnected affects—to the broader collective, rightly and persistently making their way toward demanding just social transformation.

If we recognize that the hidden and undesirable traits of the 1950s—anger, disobedience, and rebellion among many others—are buried or elbowed back into cultural shadows, then we also recognize that these same traits are slowly and steadily becoming more operational when realized and called upon—alchemizing into "gold"—in a variety of marginalized contexts. It is here, in the underdeveloped traits, characteristics, attitudes, and aptitudes of the cultural golden shadow, that the Peace Movement, writ large, senses an abundant supply of untapped affect and energy to help fuel its ongoing pursuit of resisting large-scale institutions and unjust social and cultural traditions. In the U.S. Civil Rights movement, for example, the Supreme Court's 1954 breakthrough decision to strike down racial segregation in Brown vs. Board of Education, sparks further resistance in other border zones of racial integration. The American Federation of Labor (AFL) and the Congress of Industrial Organizations (CIO) merge resources in 1955 to better back the American Labor/Union movement and together they form the AFL-CIO (AFL-CIO, n.d.). Both the women's movement and the sexual revolution advocate for the Federal Drug Administration's approval of birth control pills through reproductive freedom debates centering upon voluntary motherhood (Susan B. Anthony Center for Women's Leadership, n.d.; Planned Parenthood, n.d.). The Mattachine Society, the first modern gay rights organization, is founded in California in 1950 and gains members and political presence throughout the next 19 years—until the Stonewall riots of 1969 usher in a more radical lesbian and gay large-scale movement (Cusac, 1999). And, the U.S.'s antiwar movement begins its tenure with the formation of several influential groups across a spectrum of activists—the National Committee for a Sane Nuclear Policy (SANE), Committee for Nonviolent Action (CNVA), and Student Peace Union (SPU) to name but a few.

While this sounds decent and heroic for the groups involved in various locations of struggle, their actions are not without deep and serious risk. Any time a protest is levied against government, dominant culture, mainstream groups, or religious institutions, the threat of physical, psychological, emotional, or spiritual harm is present, as is the risk of detainment from personal freedom and liberties and corporal incarceration. For that reason, willingness to engage with the cultural shadow, which is much larger than any one individual or group, and then to choose to enter into a relationship with it in order to resurrect a potential yet enigmatic beneficent quality is no small achievement, and is not without consequence. Jung submits insight about this generally vexing experience in the following excerpt from *Aion* (1959a). (For the purpose of our analysis, the constructive aspects of the shadow are included together with the ominous aspects with which Jung marks the shadow.)

> The shadow is a moral problem that challenges the whole ego-personality, for no one can become conscious of the shadow without considerable moral effort. To become conscious of it involves recognizing the dark [and constructive] aspects of the personality as present and real. This act is the essential condition for any kind of self-knowledge, and it therefore, as a rule meets with considerable resistance. Indeed, self-knowledge as a psychotherapeutic measure frequently requires much painstaking work extending over a long period.
>
> (p. 8)

Acknowledging the risk involved in looking into and engaging with shadow and golden shadow, Miller (1989) notes that "there is an inertia in culture and subculture to retain the status quo, no matter what it is. This element is relatively unsupportive of, if not critical of nonconformity, experimentation, and risk-taking" (p. 114). As the long history of worldwide resistance movements makes clear, risk-taking in the face of governmental and entrenched institutionalized systems of constraint and hegemony tends to be the unglamorous collective task of those under the umbrella of activists, peaceworkers/makers/builders, and concerned citizens; and as such, their work is often underappreciated, undervalued, underpaid, and swept into the sidelines of society, reported on near the last page of the newspaper or at the end of the news feed. And yet, despite multitudinal and relentless obstacles, activists and peaceworkers keep working until they no longer can, the elders of each movement retire to make room for the always-present up-and-comers, and comprehensive structural change eventually materializes through enantiodromia. As we know, grand societal transformations *can* and *do* take place; they just do not take place overnight or without effort, struggle, or resistance.

Kairos—The Right Time, Place, and People

Echoing Jung's sentiments above, Miller (1989) observes in his research of great transformations and the golden shadow: "These experiences are processes wherein the emerging Golden Shadow is nourished and integrated into conscious behavior. Time and nourishment are the key ingredients" (p. 81). Dealing with the detonation of an immense cultural secret and its far-reaching psychical fallout, we, the West, needed significant time, patience, and persistence to assemble a critical mass that would consciously and willingly engage and tend to the disregarded traits manifesting in the golden shadow and risk actualizing them into action. During these years, which span more than a decade, the West labors to find a way to unearth and integrate these new potentials—anger, anxiety, fear, rebellion—into our reformulating conscious persona. Still, the desire on behalf of social movements to understand how to engage effectively with the new potentials and what to do with them at the collective level presents unique challenges to those aware of their presences.

Thus, weaving the shadow and golden shadow threads together allows us to theorize that as kairos' time and nourishment are provided, fresh discoveries emerging into consciousness offer an exclusive opportunity for self-authorized choice. For in the arduous proactive process of harvesting shadow characteristics to consciousness (golden or not), it becomes the seeker's responsibility to receive and then act upon—whether consciously or intuitively—the new options that she or he has greatly labored to bring to fruition. "Not to act," Miller shares, "is itself a choice and therefore an action. This action, which is demanded by our new awareness, is the essence of risk. *Choosing is risking, and risking is choosing*" (1989, p. 117). And in the context of intentional nonviolent peacework, of which the Campaign for Nuclear Disarmament (CND) and like-minded groups insist, there is usually more demanded of the decision to act than simply to decide whether to risk or not; the consideration of which action(s) would serve as wise, or right, action(s) are equally driving and important.

Doing Nothing Sets It Free

A week after from the shockingly successful four-day 1958 Easter march from London to Aldermaston, the Executive Committee of the three-month-old CND meets to debrief the march, and as such, the fourth item on the agenda, according to the "Minutes of the Meeting of the Executive Committee," is "Name of the Campaign and Symbol." The committee agrees on the spot to adopt the "semaphore symbol and to have window bills and car stickers [and] badges for sale, at first in the London area. The Secretary was instructed.... to make enquiries as to whether it was possible to register the name and symbol" (Campaign for Nuclear Disarmament, 1958a). Although we will investigate this further in a short while, it is important to note here that from its inception, the ND symbol, or "peace symbol," is intentionally commodified and partnered with commercialism, capitalism, and consumerism for the means of national, local, and committee fundraising efforts. And these committee members, who ratify the symbol and agree to initially seek its legal protection, are the same folks who coordinate the conditions—time and nourishment—for its eventual flourish in worldwide enterprise.

At the following Executive Committee meeting, the first order of business for the committee is "Matters Arising" with the first subheading, "Registration of Name and Symbol." Here Peggy Duff reports that a lawyer informed her that the name of the Campaign could only be registered as a private company, and the symbol could only be registered through a patent office; hence the process would be slow and expensive for a name and symbol that "were now so identified with the Campaign that an injunction could be obtained if necessary. It was agreed to do nothing" (Campaign for Nuclear Disarmament, 1958b). Thus, with both time and financial prohibitions present, the decision to *not* register or trademark the ND symbol—just one month after its debut—sets it free. The action of inaction, with the committee's full awareness of the affective efficacy the ND symbol offers its constituents essentially risks whatever outcomes will arise from releasing it into the public domain. The seemingly innocuous decision "to do nothing" actually sets in motion the differing ways the symbol is able to function and labor in the visual and cultural economy from this point forward. The symbol is now able to enact, or embody, the very principles for which it was created; it can—without restraint—resist, defy, and protest in the name of survival, peace, freedom, and justice.

In her text, *Psyche and Matter*, Von Franz (1988) reiterates, "true symbols are not invented by consciousness but are spontaneously revealed by the unconscious...... They always retain an ineffable and mysterious quality that seems to reveal to us more than we can really know" (p. 254). We will never know with certainty whether Holtom's design was invented by consciousness (as the semaphore signal origin story alludes), or whether it was spontaneously revealed by the unconscious (as the "drawing a human being in despair" origin story alludes), or both, but we do know there is something psychologically singular about the ND symbol when placed amongst others of its kind. In its formative years, and in spite of its enigmatic design that at the start meets with "it will 'never catch on'" resistance (Randle, 1986, p. 32), it exudes an inenarrable and inexplicable quality that entices enough individuals to form a critical mass and incites them to participate in intentional nonviolent direct action lobbied against government.

The ND movement would not have been *as* successful as it was if the ND symbol did not concurrently emerge with the debut of the large-scale CND marches, and vice versa. Their interdependent co-arising relationship is a prime example of the chicken and the egg maxim—they arise in mutual dependence and neither is independent. And while the CND gathers restless, eager, and enthusiastic followers at a rapid pace, it is not until after years of futile protests by smaller disparate ND groups in the early 1950s that it finally brings together, in loose solidarity, interested individuals and radical activists in a sustainable mass campaign. As the golden shadow theory enjoins, the fledgling ND movement needs to nourish the common backbone of its early failures, which sends it searching for a different appearance and ontological position, while also staunchly retaining the core values of *satyagraha* and *ahimsa*—the Sanskrit terms, or Gandhian principles, for active intentional nonviolence, resistance, or noninjury. When the qualities of chronos and kairos ultimately co-arise in Britain's particular cultural situation, the ND movement is ready and almost burgeoning beyond comfort and control; its unusual and never-seen-before circular mandala symbol materializes onto over 500 "lollypops" and banners; and the symbol is poised to herald the marches, organize the rallies, and communicate the campaign's presence to onlookers and interested media. It is indeed the right visual aid to surface at the right time, effectively shunting the muddled affect of a particular group of disparaged yet hopeful individuals toward the form and discipline of nonviolent direct action.

In many ways, these organizations' scintilla, or soul spark, is to midwife—for its current and unborn generations—a rebirth from a nuclearized normalcy into a nuclear free world. According to Jung, circular images, or more precisely mandalas, enchant because they "are birth-places, vessels of birth in the most literal sense" (1954/1959b, p. 130). Mandalas, like the ND symbol, usually express numinous or philosophical thoughts and ideas and through their mostly "intuitive, irrational character and, through their symbolic content, exert a retroactive influence on the unconscious" (Jung, 1969, p. 77). Fascinatingly, Jung asserts that mandalas possess a magical significance whose possible efficacy is never consciously felt by the viewer (p. 77), and this statement reminds us at once of Margaret Tims, who asserts in her article for *Peace News* that the first Aldermaston march and its symbol has a "kind of magic... . which caught the public imagination with extraordinary effect" (1959b, p. 2). Thus, in retrospect, it seems that as the CND fans the affective embers of hope and change and the ND symbol encapsulates and amplifies the ideological Easter motifs of death and rebirth, they likewise converge, for the active campaigner, on a psychological union of opposites. In his Foreword for W.Y. Evans

Wentz's (1954) *The Tibetan Book of the Great Liberation: The Method of Realizing Nirvana Through Knowing the World*, Jung tenders a useful rendering of the union of opposites in rebirth symbolism:

> Rebirth symbolism simply describes the union of opposites—conscious and unconscious—by means of concretistic analogies. Underlying all rebirth symbolism is the transcendent function. Since this function results in an increase of consciousness (the previous condition augmented by the addition of formerly unconscious contents), the new condition carries more insight, which is symbolized by more light (In alchemy, the philosopher's stone was called, among other things, *lux moderna, lux lucis, lumen luminum*, etc).
>
> (Jung, 1954, p. lxiv)

Not surprisingly, Jung's ideas about rebirth symbolism, or the union of opposites, are remarkably like those of the golden shadow... rebirth symbolism increases consciousness just as resurrecting discarded qualities from the shadow increases consciousness. In both cases, too, and if one is so moved, the new condition's insight allows it to transcend its previous condition, its cultural normalities, or its status quo. Individuals laboring for the CND more or less tacitly understand this matricentric wisdom for they intentionally join a campaign that correspondingly labors, with deep pains, to include unilateral ND policy in its desire to rebirth British foreign policy—an active bid to transcend the nuclearized status quo.

One means for campaigners to indicate their profound support of the campaign's mission and political climate presence is to informally and formally scrawl, chalk, draw, erect, graffiti, and print the CND's customized and tailored mandala anywhere and everywhere they can. For this reason, the ND symbol's *active participation* in a wide array of meaningful events becomes its essential definition, to the exclusion of those characteristics that it shares with other peace symbols. While this "graphic may hold idiosyncrasies that lend itself to inclusion in the meaningful event," in our case, the first Aldermaston march (with Holtom's ability to "sell" the symbol to CND leadership and their ability to immediately receive and accept it, for instance), its capacity to catalyze and to siphon "the energies of the tribe lies in the fact that for a particular time and place the expectations of the participants and the idiosyncrasies of the image coalesced in such a way as to create *meaning*" (Van Eenwyk, 1997, p. 82).

How did the ND symbol play a role in stimulating the comprehensive Peace Movement? To help with this, we once again turn to Peggy Duff, who possesses a keen and sharp understanding of how the ND symbol functions not only in the CND movement, but also as it begins to accumulate cultural capital in the visual economy around the globe. The following observations, made during and after her tenure with the Campaign, are of the wide array of ways the ND symbol serves the diverse movements associated with it. These are her unparaphrased reflections as recorded in her autobiography, *Left, Left, Left* (1971):

- We put it on badges, on leaflets, on posters, on notepaper, on flags and on banners. And most of all we put it on walls, for it was ideal for graffiti—so easy to draw, so quick to paint on a wall. I have found it all over world.

  (p. 116)

- For a long time it stayed black and white, as Gerald wanted it. Later on, though I still went on fighting his battle, it turned up in pinks, greens, blue, golds and orange and in every colour of the spectrum. But it was never so good as black and white, stark and simple. And for many years we kept the colours for our leaflets and banners and posters, so that the style, the symbol and the colours became the hallmark of the campaign.

  (p. 116)

- Designers loved it. They took it and played with it, made it tiny and enormous, twisted it, cut pieces off of it, but always it was unmistakable.

  (p. 116)

- It defeated the powers-that-be of London Transport. They would never accept political slogans on posters. Yet the symbol said nothing overtly, though everyone knew what it meant. Year after year it passed their censors and politicized the posters, put the message across.

(p. 116)

- It was a free for all, because while there were some who would like to have patented it, restricted its use to the respectable and acceptable people, this was never possible because it wasn't ours. It was first produced for that *ad hoc* committee which organized the first Aldermaston March. It was used by the CND, by the Direct Action Committee, the Committee of 100, the Independent Nuclear Disarmament Election Committee, by all the ad hoc groups.

(p. 117)

- It outgrew the campaign and outlived many campaigners as it travelled around the world. It became a symbol of protest, of defiance, of resistance.

(p. 117)

- We learned to accept the contribution that people had to make. Designers who made us our posters were given a free hand, although there were always some on a committee who wanted to alter them, who disliked the designs.... . If we had tried to make them conform, it would have been a different sort of a movement.

(pp. 209–210)

Kairos, the suitable confluence of emergent time, conditions and nourishment, seems to have captured the sparking of affective matrices, emergent golden shadow qualities, and a shepherding ND symbol that ignited individuals into action, and at a certain critical mass, launched the much larger campaign into global politics—with much gusto, charisma, and fanfare. To accomplish this undertaking, however, the CND would have to understand, at some level, its singular novel offering to the British populace. Unlike any other opportunity beforehand, the Campaign grants the concerned individual British citizen front row access to the rousing edge of political revolution, all while contemporaneously being housed within the safety and privacy of mass movement anonymity. With this type of allure and success, this method of mass public resistance does not stay in England for long.

The Peace Symbol Immigrates to the U.S.

Times of cultural change or revolutions are often turbulent times of experimentation, rule-breaking, and launching inventive ideas or innovative ways of doing things. This aligns with Miller's (1989) observations that the

> experience of living out the discovered dimensions of our Golden Shadow requires us to take risks and stretch ourselves. We reach beyond our grasp, and we risk failure each time we do it. It is, nevertheless, in this mind-set and atmosphere that creativity occurs.
>
> (p. 138)

We see how this applies to the late 1950s and early 1960s when the U.S.'s Peace Movement, as a collection of divergent and convergent organizing campaigns, provides individuals the opportunity to directly and deeply engage with the psychological constructs of *possibility* and *creativity*. The Peace Movement also offers kairos or the well-timed opportunity for individuals to participate in and embody—all under the cloak of anonymity in mass movement—*strategic structural change*. The ability, then, of mass social movements to graft an individual's concerns onto the collective's concerns through the modalities of protesting, defiance, and resistance is, for the individual and reciprocally for the mass movement, profoundly powerful and transcendental.

> He told us what the symbol meant. First, the semaphore for the initials, ND. Second, the broken cross meant the death of man, the circle the unborn child. It represented the threat of nuclear weapons to all mankind, and because this was new, the threat to the unborn child. He "sold" us the symbol that night.
>
> (Duff, 1971, p. 115)

Duff's retelling of her first encounter with the ND symbol aligns with how Holtom presents the symbol's meaning in his 1961 article, "The ND Symbol." Holtom writes that an assistant named Eric Austen compiled research on the "origins of symbolism" that reveals that Holtom's little man in despair *is* the gesture of despair, a "motif [that] has been associated throughout ancient history with 'the death of man,' and the circle with 'the unborn child.' The significance of the two motifs combined is the predicament in which, by chance, we live" (p. 6). It is also, by chance, that by which the ND symbol is meaningful and effectual to the co-arising movements across the Atlantic Ocean in the U.S.—civil rights, women's rights, labor union rights, poverty, unemployment, lesbian and gay rights, anti-war and military draft—and by which it blossoms into the mantling "peace symbol."

Several intrinsic traits allow the peace symbol to morph beyond the ad hoc marches into an unboundaried cultural object. Broadly stated, they are the ability to (1) transcend languages and borders, (2) to be immediately present in diverse locations of struggle, and (3) to occupy important and varied functions and meanings for the groups and individuals who make use of it. More explicitly, though, the peace symbol functions as a conduit to help organize the abundance of disconnected images, ideas, and disordered affect of the chaotic collective radioactive psyche in the late 1950s and the 1960s. When asking the following question, "How does the peace symbol function in the liberation movements associated with it?" the following nine nonordinal-ranked themes surface. When the peace symbol is present, it is (1) *requesting* future action or direct action from the organization's constituents and interested others, (2) *demonstrating* direct action-in-the-moment and the presence of the organization to onlookers, (3) *utilizing* its cultural capital to draw attention to Unilateral Nuclear Disarmament (UND), ND, or kindred issues, (4) *advocating* for a position on domestic or foreign policy, (5) *offering* interested individuals or groups the opportunity to join and engage with the movement, (6) *supporting* or taking responsibility for a current or past action or event, (7) *transcending* local languages, (8) *indicating* available resources to those active in the movement, or (9) *raising* funds.

There are, of course, additional uses and functions of the peace symbol, but they are not main themes or patterns. The nine themes are discussed below, with one or two representative primary source data photographs for each.

Requesting Future Action or Direct Action from the Organization's Constituents and Interested Others

While presenting much content and details about the event, each flyer takes care to include the peace symbol as a visual cue to the onlooker about what type of action may be asked for and by whom. The first flyer (Figure 4.3) from 1962 calls students to join the SPU, "to converge on Washington.... to demonstrate before U.S. Government offices and the Soviet Embassy to make clear their demand for an end to nuclear testing, an end to fraudulent civil defense, and a beginning of concrete initiatives for peace." The flyer concludes with an affective appeal to the student viewer, "This is our chance to make ourselves a political force which cannot be ignored."

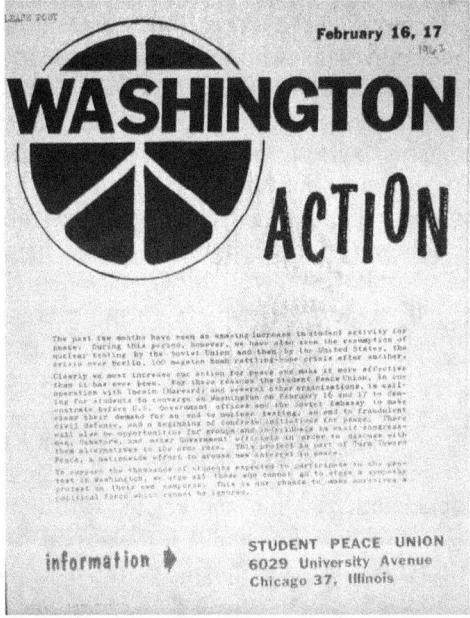

Figure 4.3 Washington Action, February 16, 17, 1962. Retrieved from Student Peace Union Archive Records (DG 65, Box 2), Swarthmore College Peace Collection, Swarthmore, PA. With Permission: Swarthmore College Peace Collection, Swarthmore, PA.

Kairos 99

From the CND's archives, Figure 4.4 is an operative example of one of Peggy Duff's observations about the ND symbol cited earlier in this chapter: "Designers loved it. They took it and played with it, made it tiny and enormous, twisted it, cut pieces off of it, but always it was unmistakable" (1971, p. 116). Indeed, with approximately one-third of the symbol missing, it is still immediately clear to the viewer which symbol is indicated in the poster and what sorts of topics may be covered in a rally by the somewhat nebulous title of "Signpost to a Sane World." Steadfast to Gerald Holtom's prescription of black and white colors, the symbol is visibly clear from quite a distance, it easily

Figure 4.4 Signpost to a Sane World, 1962. Retrieved from Campaign for Nuclear Disarmament Archive Records (CDG-B, Reel 132.10, LSE 5/19), Swarthmore College Peace Collection, Swarthmore, PA. With Permission: Swarthmore College Peace Collection, Swarthmore, PA.

communicates the campaign's presence and intentions to the viewer, and it requests future action from its constituents and interested others.

Demonstrating Direct Action-in-the-Moment and the Presence of the Organization to Onlookers

Figure 4.5 shows a view from nonviolent direct action occurring in front of the New York Federal District Courthouse, and the synopsis on the backside of the photo says the convened group is

> protesting against the detention of crew members of "Everyman," a boat bound to the Pacific area where the United States are carrying [on] their nuclear tests. The trip was intended to be a dramatic appeal against the dangerous experiments and in favor of world peace and general disarmament. Many American women participated.

Figure 4.5 Everyman I-CNVA, 1962. Retrieved from WIN Magazine Photograph Records (DG 77, Box 5), Swarthmore College Peace Collection, Swarthmore, PA. With Permission: Swarthmore College Peace Collection, Swarthmore, PA.

Figure 4.6 represents a "sitdown" organized by the CNVA. This group of nonviolent demonstrators is seated outside of the Atomic Energy Commission's (AEC) headquarters to protest—through acts of civil disobedience—the AEC's promotion of nuclear energy production. At the time of this January 30, 1962 sitdown, the AEC was responsible for the U.S.'s ongoing underground nuclear weapons testing and also threatened to resume atmospheric testing in the Pacific Ocean (Buck, 1983, p. 4). This photograph clearly shows the function of the peace symbol as demonstrating direct action-in-the-moment and the presence of the organization to onlookers. The viewer's eye is pulled toward the striking peace symbol that is intentionally overlayed onto an already existing placard with text. The overpowering prominence of the peace symbol suggests that the protester understood that the symbol's presence communicated *more* and communicated it more effectively to onlookers than what the original text could hope to do.

In these demonstrations, the presence of the peace symbol indicates to curious onlookers that direct action is happening in the present moment. In that same moment it also challenges

Figure 4.6 Atomic Energy Commission Sitdown, January 30, 1962. Retrieved from WIN Magazine Photographs Records (DG 77, Box 4), Swarthmore College Peace Collection, Swarthmore, PA. With Permission: Swarthmore College Peace Collection, Swarthmore, PA.

onlookers to make a choice—will they join the protest to publicly affirm their beliefs and convictions? Will they leave the area and oppose or disengage from the principles of the mass social movement? Or, will they choose the betwixt and between role of spectator, of one who passively participates from the sidelines? In any of these cases, when nonviolent direct action is happening in the public sphere, onlookers are confronted to think about and reflect upon the issue at hand as they are required to make a choice about whether to engage, disengage, or become a voyeur without much effect.

Utilizing its Cultural Capital to Draw Attention to UND, ND, or Kindred Issues

The peace symbol's third function is one that is initially unique to the U.S. For, when the symbol is used primarily by the CND in England, it acts more like an emblem for the lone issue of UND— a figured object used with symbolic meaning, as the distinctive badge of a person, family, nation, etc. (Emblem, n.d.). In the U.S., however, the symbol is almost immediately linked to myriad social justice issues by groups like the more panoptic CNVA and the SPU. Figure 4.7 is a flyer from 1961 that simultaneously labors on several different semiotic levels. First, it shows the onlooker what the CNVA's Peace Walk from San Francisco to Moscow March—a nonviolent direct action march—looks like; second, it includes the peace symbol in action, out on the streets, hoisted on lollypops and placards (function 2); third, it uses the peace symbol to draw attention to a scheduled assembly to hear the leader of the transcontinental walk, Brad Lyttle, speak (function 1); and lastly, the flyer indicates that a collection will be taken for walk expenses (function 9).

Figure 4.8 is from one of the many CNVA sponsored long-distance walks. The photo notes have some tentative notations about its identification, but they indicate that the photo was most likely taken in Florida during the peace walk from Quebec, Canada through to Washington D.C. and on to Guantanamo Bay, Cuba. The Quebec–Washington–Guantanamo Bay Walk for Peace and Freedom is an integrated walk protesting *for* racial integration and *against* U.S. actions in Cuba at the same time.

Figure 4.7 Peace Walk: San Francisco to Moscow, 1961. Retrieved from Student Peace Union Archive Records (DG 65, Box 2), Swarthmore College Peace Collection, Swarthmore, PA. With Permission: Swarthmore College Peace Collection, Swarthmore, PA.

Advocating for a Position on Domestic or Foreign Policy

As the peace symbol's ontological position expands, it is able to incorporate emergent social issues and labor on their behalf. Figure 4.9 shows a CNVA brochure aimed at raising awareness and inviting action against the Internal Revenue Service's Telephone War Tax. The mythically provocative cover image presents the winged figure of Hermes, god of communication and the messenger for all the gods, standing upon a globe (western hemisphere represented) with telephone cables wrapped around him, harkening the image of the healing one-snake medicinal

104 Kairos

Figure 4.8 Unidentified Photos, May, 1963. Retrieved from WIN Magazine Photograph Records (DG 77, Box 5), Swarthmore College Peace Collection, Swarthmore, PA. Copyright Permission granted by Swarthmore College Peace Collection, Swarthmore, PA. With Permission: Swarthmore College Peace Collection, Swarthmore, PA.

caduceus of Hippocrates or the lesser known two-snake caduceus of Hermes—an iconographical representation of peace (Morford & Lenardon, 1995). In his left hand he holds a peace symbol that is approximate in size to the globe, and in his right hand he holds the single torn and frazzled end of a telephone cable. While every pressure letter campaign, protest, or demonstration advocates, at its core, for a change in domestic or foreign policies, some issues, such as the Telephone War Tax Refusal Campaign are less prominent or publicized than ND or civil rights, and as such this brochure is exemplary of highlighting the efficacy of the peace symbol's fourth function.

On August 30, 1965, Lyndon B. Johnson signed into law a new act making men who willingly destroy their draft cards subject

Figure 4.9 Hang Up on War, 1966. Retrieved from Committee for Nonviolent Action Archive Records (DG 017, Box 2), Swarthmore College Peace Collection, Swarthmore, PA. With Permission: Swarthmore College Peace Collection, Swarthmore, PA.

to five years in prison and/or a $10,000 fine. These were the same consequences of 1948's Federal Law requiring all men over 18 and born after 1922 to carry a draft card. The critical significance of draft cards, according to the flyer in Figure 4.10, is that they are the only document in American history "that tens of millions must either carry or face the courts and a five-year maximum sentence." Further still, the psychological implications of carrying federal draft cards are that they represent "the symbolic link between every young American and the present war." Figure 4.10 is a photograph of a CNVA flyer advocating civil disobedience as a defiance response to a system of interlocked domestic and foreign policies requiring the draft. The center point of our inquiry, the peace symbol, is placed in the upper left hand corner, the paramount position of importance for Western readers. The symbol stands alone, unhindered, and in its most effective colors—black and white. From this preeminent position, the peace symbol provides a context for the

Figure 4.10 Burn Draft Cards-Not People, 1965. Retrieved from Committee for Nonviolent Action Archive Records (DG 017, Box 2), Swarthmore College Peace Collection, Swarthmore, PA. With Permission: Swarthmore College Peace Collection, Swarthmore, PA.

rest of the flyer and efficaciously advocates for increased awareness and action against unjust domestic and foreign policies.

Offering Interested Individuals or Groups the Opportunity to Join and Engage with the Movement

For recruitment purposes, the peace symbol bodes well. By the time it reaches the U.S. from Great Britain, it has already found its way onto badges, buttons, bumper stickers, window and car bills, jewelry, clothing, and more, and, despite the odds, it is becoming a counter-culture fashion statement (how often do politics and fashion mix and become available to the masses?). The symbol's fifth function, offering the opportunity to join and engage the movement, often comes along with wearing a peace symbol on your person or vehicle, and hoisting the peace symbol up on a lollypop, banner, or placard. Other times, the symbol is utilized to offer opportunities to "Join" or "Support" an organization (Figures 4.11), and it effectively recruits for multiple levels of engagement: from direct action, field projects, work and

Figure 4.11 September 18, 1959, p. 6. With Permission: Peace News, London, Britain. PeaceNews.info

study programs, to volunteerism, speakers, trainers, canvassers, and listening participants. Likewise, the placard at the center of Figure 4.11 says, "Walk With Us Next Time," which is an attention-grabbing tactic that allows the onlooker to ingest the seed of suggestion, mull and gestate the idea, work through any tentativeness, apathy, or discomfort, and make a personal decision beforehand about whether to join the organization or demonstration at the next opportunity.

Supporting or Taking Responsibility for a Current or Past Action or Event

Oftentimes, the peace symbol functions as a marker to onlookers that the organization supports individual activism of the direct action-in-the-moment type (function 2). It supplies onlookers with a context for the somewhat arcane action happening beside it. Without the peace symbol's presence, it would likewise be unclear whether the occasion was a demonstration against local issues, national, or foreign policy, or something else altogether. In Figure 4.12, for example, *The Spirit of Freedom* is one of several boats used by the CNVA to commit civil disobedience acts to protest against domestic and foreign policies. In this instance, *The Spirit of Freedom* was employed to transport marchers of the Quebec–Washington-Guantanamo Bay Walk for Peace and Freedom from Miami, FL to Cuba. However, the U.S. confiscated

Figure 4.12 The Spirit of Freedom. Retrieved from WIN Magazine Photos (DG 77, Box 5), Swarthmore College Peace Collection, Swarthmore, PA. With Permission: Swarthmore College Peace Collection, Swarthmore, PA.

the boat, citing the recent commercial, economic, financial, and travel embargo against Cuba. Not only were the activists using *The Spirit of Freedom*—with the peace symbol also painted on its bow—to draw attention to and urge for UND and nonviolent defense policies, but to also speak "out against militarism by all nations and [suggest] nonviolent alternatives which could be the basis of world peace and freedom" (Committee for Nonviolent Action, 1964, July). These principles underscored their main objective for this specific protest—to advocate for a change in the federal restrictions for free and open travel for the common U.S. citizen to Cuba.

For readers of newsprint, photo journalizing the peace symbol plays an important role in attracting the potential reader to the article at hand. Figure 4.13 is a picture of July 3, 1962 article in the

Figure 4.13 Peace and Integration, July 3, 1962. Retrieved from Committee For Nonviolent Action Archive Records (DG 017, Box C13 CNVA Bulletin 1960–1966), Swarthmore College Peace Collection, Swarthmore, PA. With Permission: Swarthmore College Peace Collection, Swarthmore, PA.

CNVA Bulletin showing a mixed group of student peacewalkers and student leaders of the "integration movement" (p. 4). On bended knee whilst taking a respite from walking to pose for a photograph, the standard bearer leans on the wooden lath bearing the peace symbol. As we have already mentioned in previous photos, the peace symbol, perched high, is working simultaneously on different registers. However, Figure 4.13 is an excellent example in which to spotlight the sixth function—taking responsibility for a past action. This function is born from a public relations stance, one that requires organizations to take credit for upcoming or past events in order to increase visibility, legibility, and publicity of their mission and causes at hand.

Transcending Local Languages

One of the interesting upshots from the CNVA's grueling and expensive transcontinental and transnational marches is that they literally carried the symbol, in the context it was originally designed for, over country and cultural borders repeatedly (Figure 4.14). The symbol easily slips from one location to the next, clothed in local languages to maximize the effectiveness of the march's presence and message. Along the way, local peace chapters welcome the marchers and provide prefabricated placards, banners, and lollypops, as well as leaflets and pamphlets in local languages

Figure 4.14 1961: For East-West Peace. Retrieved from Committee for Nonviolent Action Archive Records (DG 017, Box 2), Swarthmore College Peace Collection, Swarthmore, PA. With Permission: Swarthmore College Peace Collection, Swarthmore, PA.

Figure 4.15 1962–Aldermaston International Banners. Original photograph copyright Campaign for Nuclear Disarmament, London, England. With Permission: cnduk.org

to increase peace-full one-on-one interactions with local citizens. For this reason, it is the actual activists themselves, and not necessarily once-removed commercialism or capitalism that carry and disseminate the peace symbol into countries of North America, Africa, and Europe during the late 1950s and early 1960s.

Figures 4.15 is a standard image of the peace symbol being used in a way to transmit an idea, message, or presence to onlookers who may not speak local languages. Without the symbol's presence, a foreign onlooker or consumer of the media would not know what to make of the march.

Indicating Available Resources to Those Active in the Movement

In the early years of the CND, houses and businesses along the Aldermaston march route hung sheets, cloths, or window bills emblazoned with the symbol to signify to the Aldermaston marchers that theirs is a safe place offering support in the form of respite and hospitality. Likewise, cars displaying the symbol offer lifts to some of the campaigners or offer to run errands or logistics for them along the march's route. In an international context, the symbol serves as visual "passport" of sorts for walkers in unfamiliar locations to seek out like-minded organizations for fellowship and for securing resources (Duff, 1971). Other ways that the peace symbol indicates resources to those in the movement or to those interested in joining the movement are exemplified in Figures 4.16 and 4.17. Figure 4.16 is a basic membership brochure for the SPU in 1961. Inside the brochure one can find information about the history, mission, structure, actions, steps to join the organization (function 5), and the benefits/resources of membership. Figure 4.17 shows a tri-fold leaflet with the peace symbol on its cover with the words "CNVA Literature List" embedded within the lines of the symbol. The leaflet's intention is to indicate

Figure 4.16 Student Peace Union Membership Brochure, 1961. Retrieved from Student Peace Union Archive Records (DG 65, Box 2). Swarthmore College Peace Collection, Swarthmore, PA. With Permission: Swarthmore College Peace Collection, Swarthmore, PA.

Figure 4.17 CNVA Literature List, 9/63. Retrieved from Committee For Nonviolent Action Archive Records (DG 017, Box 2), Swarthmore College Peace Collection, Swarthmore, PA. With Permission: Swarthmore College Peace Collection, Swarthmore, PA.

to those who are seeking more information that a resource list of educational literature produce by the CNVA and about its projects during the years 1958–1963 is provided inside.

Raising Funds

Lastly, but certainly not less important, is the utilization of the peace symbol as a means of self-generating financial support for ongoing projects and organizational costs. Whether it was through badges, lapel buttons, earrings, tie tacks, stickers, key chains, or any of the promotional items found in "Brown's Peace Aids: A Non-Profit Service Supplying Educational and Promotional Aids for the Peace Movement" (Brown's Peace Aids, 1964), any organization within the Peace Movement could not do its work without

114 Kairos

extensive fundraising efforts. Figure 4.18 is an instructive example of the peace symbol's distinguished recognizability and psychological import when placed next to other symbols of the Peace Movement. One interesting note about the composition of the peace symbol is that it is at its best when the circle around the "human being in despair" is of the same color and width as the figure. Notice the first peace symbol button in the first column, and then notice the ones in the second column. While their shape and form is evident, the second column buttons visually lose some of their impact when the human figure is not specifically contained within a space (temenos) that the graphic, itself, makes. Yes, the human figure is contained within the perimeter of the object's

Figure 4.18 Peace Pins and Jewelry, 1964 Retrieved from Student Peace Union Archive Records (DG 65, Box 1), Swarthmore College Peace Collection, Swarthmore, PA. With Permission: Swarthmore College Peace Collection, Swarthmore, PA.

space, yet conceptually, it does not offer quite the same impact as does the image containing itself. In this second version, it looks more like the popular "chicken foot" or "upside down broken cross" critiques often put forth against the symbol.

While tracking the peace symbol's birth and development, first in Britain and then in the U.S., one of the more striking revelations to emerge from the data is that the symbol is most effective when in immediate human contact. An active march lollypop, which labors on behalf of the purpose for which it was designed, for instance, is much more affectively effective to an onlooker than a symbol-bearing press release or letterhead. Because the symbol—initially supported by surrounding text and slogans on banners and placards in energetic environments—is able to mirror the physical form and affect of the activists who raise it and the onlookers who interpret it, at very deep, unconscious, and symbolic levels, its resonance is such that the collective and the individual infuse it with ambitious meaning. As the fusion of affect, energy, and meaning pour into the budding Peace Movement, it fuels the symbol's efficacy to shift and adapt as it labors for myriad causes on behalf of organizations and individuals. In reciprocal and co-arising fashion, individuals are likewise drawn to labor on behalf of the ideals, purpose, and possibilities offered by the Peace Movement and its symbol.

References

AFL-CIO. (n.d.). Our labor history timeline. Retrieved from https://aflcio.org/about-us/history

Brown's Peace Aids. (1964). Student Peace Union Archives (DG 65, Box 1). Swarthmore College Peace Collection, Swarthmore, PA.

Buck, A. L. (1983). A history of the Atomic Energy Commission (DOE/ES-0003/1). Washington, DC: U. S. Department of Energy.

Campaign for Nuclear Disarmament, (1958a, April 14). Minutes of the Meeting of the Executive Committee [Microfilm edition]. Campaign for Nuclear Disarmament Archives (Reel 132.1, w1/7). Swarthmore College Peace Collection, Swarthmore, PA.

Campaign for Nuclear Disarmament. (1958b, May 6). Minutes of the Meeting of the Executive Committee [Microfilm edition]. Campaign for Nuclear Disarmament Archives (Reel 132.1, w1/8). Swarthmore College Peace Collection, Swarthmore, PA.

CNVA Bulletin. (1962, July 3). Peace and integration. Committee for Nonviolent Action Archives (DG 017, Box C13 CNVA Bulletin 1960–1966). Swarthmore College Peace Collection, Swarthmore PA.

Committee for Nonviolent Action (1964, July). Mark Morris presents a benefit for the Committee for Nonviolent Action's Quebec-Washington-Guantanamo Walk for Peace. Committee for Nonviolent Action Archives (DG 017, Box 2). Swarthmore College Peace Collection, Swarthmore, PA.

Cusac, A. M. (1999, September). Harry Hay interview. Retrieved from www.progressive.org/mag_cusachay

Duff, P. (1971). *Left, left, left: A personal account of six protest campaigns 1945–1965.* London, England: Allison & Busby.

Emblem. (n.d.). In *Oxford English dictionary online*. Retrieved from www-oed-com.ezproxy.rollins.edu/view/Entry/60880

Holtom, G. (1961, June 2). The ND symbol. Peace News: The International Pacifist Weekly, p. 6.

Jung, C. G. (1954). Foreword: A psychological commentary. In W.Y. Evans Wentz (Ed.), *The Tibetan book of the great liberation: The method of realizing Nirvana through knowing the world* (pp. xxix–lxiv). London, England: Oxford University Press.

Jung, C. G. (1959a). *Aion*. Princeton, NJ: Princeton University Press.

Jung, C. G. (1959b). Archetypes of the collective unconscious (R. F. C. Hull, Trans.). In H. Read et al. (Series Eds.), *The collected works of C. G. Jung* (Vol. 9i, pp. 3–41). Princeton, NJ: Bollingen/Princeton University Press. (Original work published 1954).

Jung, C. G. (1969). *Mandala symbolism*. Princeton, NJ: Princeton University Press.

Lazarus, E. (1883). The new colossus. Retrieved from www.nps.gov/stli/learn/historyculture/colossus.htm

Miller, W. A. (1989). *Your golden shadow: Discovering and fulfilling your undeveloped self.* San Francisco, CA: Harper & Row.

Morford, M. P. O. & Lenardon, R. J. (1995). *Classical mythology*. White Plains, NY: Longman.

Nhat Hanh, T. (1988). *The heart of understanding*. Berkeley, CA: Parallax Press.

Planned Parenthood. (n.d.). Our History. Retrieved from www.plannedparenthood.org/about-us/who-we-are/our-history

Randle, M. (1986). Pacifism, war resistance, and the struggle against nuclear weapons: Part I: From conscientious objection to nonviolent resistance. In G. Chester & A. Rigby (Eds.), *Articles of peace: Celebrating fifty years of Peace News* (pp. 27–36). Bridport, Dorset: Prism Press.

Shepherd, R., & Shepherd, R. (2002). *1,000 symbols: What shapes mean in art and myth*. New York, NY: Thames & Hudson.

Susan B. Anthony Center for Women's Leadership. (n.d.). US Suffrage Movement timeline, 1869 to present. Retrieved from www.rochester.edu/sba/suffrage-history/us-suffrage-movement-timeline-1792-to-present/

Tims, M. (1959, June 26). ND and the Artist. *Peace News: The International Pacifist Weekly*, p. 2.
Van Eenwyk, J. R. (1997). *Archetypes and strange attractors: The chaotic world of symbols.* Toronto: Inner City Books.
Von Franz, M-L. (1988). *Psyche and matter.* Boston, MA: Shambhala.
Zweig, C., & Abrams, J. (Eds.). (1991). *Meeting the shadow: The hidden power of the dark side of human nature.* New York, NY: Jeremy Tarcher/ Penguin.

Conclusion
Today's Relevance

Rollo May (1962), a U.S. existential and humanistic psychologist, posits that every society has within it formative principles that manifest in basic symbols and myths. These symbols and myths lend form and unity to culture, which, in turn, also infuse every aspect of that culture. He writes, "symbols are the culture's form of transcending the immediate situation: they will always be bound up with the fundamental values and goals accepted in the society" (p. 4). In the West's aborning 1950s antinuclear/peace movement, the values and goals of resistance, defiance, and protest are bound up with the fundamental values and goals of survival, freedom, and peace (freedom from nuclear peril for current and future generations and peace in a broad sense of transnational and ethical responsibility). When kairos, the exact moment when large-scale nonviolent resistance hooks the intrigue, imagination, and devotion of the nuclear disarmament (ND) movement, the ND symbol emerges too, heralding the CND's agenda, shunting the pooling individual and collective affect of fear, anxiety, and anger toward nonviolent action, toward transcending the immediate situation, and toward *possibilities* in precarious times.

The public debut of the peace symbol on Easter weekend 1958 in London's Trafalgar Square embeds it as a vital node within the ND web of *active* mass resistance, defiance, and protest. At the same time, the peace symbol emerges as a fundamental nodal point within the 20th-century psychical web of Western symbol, myth, and archetype; surfaced to prominence through the psychologically dynamic *shadow-enantiodromia-kairos-golden shadow* processes of the West. This confluence of highly charged webs and psychical processes shapes and extends the peace symbol's original

DOI: 10.4324/b23325-6

Conclusion 119

meaning articulated by its creator as a representation of "a human being in despair" protesting against nuclear proliferation (Holtom, 1961, p. 6). Indeed, within two years of its debut, the peace symbol rapidly transfigures into a mantle-like cultural interface between psyche and matter, one that mediates "between consciousness and the unconscious by participating in both," as Van Eenwyk suggests all symbols do (1997, p. 111). Thus, it is the peace symbol's active participation in events, not simply its use in print media as a brand or logo, that imbues it with a particular meaning, for a particular group of people, at a particular time in Western history. Indeed, the particularities of the peace movement are historically significant, according to peace activist Andrew Rigby (1986), in that the CND, its platforms, and its popular nonviolent resistance modalities were founded, and subsequently rooted and grounded, as a *peace-time* social movement in the West (i.e., wide-spread and sustained protest during a span of militarized-defined peace).

The psychological and cultural import of the peace movement's coupling of nonviolent direct action with the ND/peace symbol at mass crowd gatherings and for the media cannot be overstated. For it is precisely this operant conditioning of *concrete action* with *abstract symbol* that encourages the peace movement to gain traction and flourish in the consciousness and visual memory of the West, working fastidiously to upend what Meador (2000) calls the severe, restrictive, and "unrealistic morality" of the preceding decades (p. 45). The unrealistic morality to which Meador refers also houses within it the repressed and oppressed constructive cultural characteristics or traits we identify as the *golden shadow*. Thus, dwelling in the collective subconscious or unconscious are constructive and underdeveloped characteristics and affects which are realized by several peace and justice activist groups to be veritable gold mines of positive and useful traits that can be nourished to effect and re-potentiate social change.

To further illustrate this point, it is widely known that the West has a strong proclivity to encourage, support, and reward extraversion in its citizens. The West likewise prizes human beings who fulfill their social roles in gregarious, companionable, and congenial ways (Miller, 1989, p. 40). "Children," Miller offers, "are prompted to be 'outgoing,' to be sociable, to mingle with others" and when children grow into adults, society implicitly stipulates "we ought to be doing something rather than 'sitting contemplating' (as though sitting contemplating were doing nothing.)" (p. 41). In the late 1950s, the ND/peace movement gathers fortitude and, in a strategic uroborous-like maneuver, transforms the dominant culture values of outgoingness, gregariousness, kindness, amiability, congeniality, sociability, and gathering with others into iconoclastic gestures of anti-government mass marches, rallies, sit-downs, and sit-ins. From a psychological perspective, this seems to create values discord and moral turmoil for mainstream society as it witnesses its own principles being turned inside out and upside down upon itself. How can society negate the social values of the peace movement while at the same time teach these same social values to its children?

Unable to hold the reality of this deep ideological and enantiodromian dissonance, the 1960s burst open, which, as Meador writes:

> exposed the cracks in the idealized hero and the virginal maiden … These events were the first widespread cultural announcement of the end of an era and the beginning of a new underlying mythology. The spontaneous eruption of a worldview genuinely counter to the prevailing culture was fueled by an eruption from the unconscious of the long-repressed contents.
> (2000, p. 56)

In our case study, the fissure wedging between thinly veiled societal control and institutionalized structures widens just enough for a rupture of untapped creative potentials—golden shadow traits—to spill over onto the front pages of the daily newspapers and to make a splattering onto the evening news. Ironically, these "disruptive" dynamics, actions, and resistance maneuvers of the CND, DAC, CNVA, and SPU look much different than the citizen of the late 1950s or early 1960s might have expected. Large masses of people collectively walking and sitting, collectively marching and chanting, collectively working and singing, collectively acting and raising their voice in resistance and protest; all together peace-fully and holding firm to the principles of nonviolence (except for cases of police brutality and harassment (Earl, Soule, & McCarthy, 2003). With careful and deliberate nourishment, development, and refinement, the golden shadow traits become, and are eventually remembered as, the hallmark actions and modalities of the West's larger peace movement.

To help demystify the peace symbol's ability to operate so powerfully in relation to social movements in the late 1950s and early 1960s, the depth psychological approach of "seeing through" or psychologizing—a way of understanding that considers a situation, event, or idea to be primarily a manifestation of the psyche was utilized (Hillman, 1975, p. 118). In our case study, in other words, there were ineffable qualities about the peace movement, its people, its actions, its style, and specifically in its symbol, that were extraordinarily appealing to large segments of the population; so much so that thousands of ordinary people were encouraged to give up their weekends or holidays to "step off the pavement and join it" (Duff, 1971, p. 132). As we discussed in Part IV, the anonymity of joining a mass movement, the sense of belonging, of no longer feeling isolated, of having shared values normalized and validated galvanized an individual's sense of agency around the heavily bureaucratic, institutionalized, and militarized social issue of ND. Thus, it is in the peace movement's utilization of, and capitalization on, dominant culture values in ways that twist them around and juxtapose them back onto the culture that gave the movement its edge, its novelty, its draw. As Rigby (1986) recalls, the "experience of direct action against the nuclear threat" had "people *acting*, refusing to be passive, seeking to participate in the determination of their future" (p. 17). And in the case of the peace symbol itself, its edge, its novelty, its draw was in part, that it was able, as Rollo May (1962) also contends on behalf of symbols in general, "to transcend the immediate concrete situation, to abstract, to think and live in terms of 'the possible'" (p. 3)—in this case the possibility of survival.

Once the symbol loosens its moorings from the British mainland and immigrates to the U.S., its adoption by activist organizations broadens its social justice agendas. The peace symbol's capacity to stand in for or represent protest, defiance, and resistance for myriad social issues outreaches its initial employ by the ad hoc London-to-Aldermaston march. However, as an unboundaried cultural object, it is able to transcend local languages and national borders, to be immediately present in diverse locations of struggle, and to occupy important and varied functions and meanings for the groups and individuals who make use of it. Because of these distinctive qualities, other countries around the world that not only have a stake in nuclear proliferation/ND polemics but also in other peace and justice polemics, likewise import the ND symbol to attend to the symbolic needs of their local active nonviolence resistances. It is during this time, the early to mid-1960s, that the ND symbol irreversibly blossoms into the "peace symbol."

The peace symbol's lack of copyright, its simple and effective graphic design, and its ability to represent varied social injustices has allowed it to remain relevant for years. However, like many things imbued with significant power and purpose that also work on behalf of those who are oppressed and suffering, the symbol has been exploited and co-opted by greed and capitalism. The CND, which is still operational today and has a vibrant presence on the World Wide Web, acknowledges the vast misuse of the symbol:

> Although specifically designed for the anti-nuclear movement it has quite deliberately never been copyrighted. No one has to pay or to seek permission before they use it. A symbol of freedom, it is free for all. This of course sometimes leads to its use, or misuse, in circumstances that CND and the peace movement find distasteful. It is also often exploited for commercial, advertising or generally fashion purposes. We can't stop this happening and have no intention of copyrighting it. All we can do is to ask commercial users if they would like to make a donation. Any money received is used for CND's peace education and information work.
> (Campaign for Nuclear Disarmament, n.d.)

As a depth psychologist, however, I theorize about whether the ND movement's sense of failure, that, in the end, it was not able to successfully lobby for unilateralism and nonproliferation, and in fact, that the proliferation of nuclear energy and weapons expanded to include a wider net of radioactive countries, has had profound implications on the power of the symbol itself. In other words, what does it mean for the symbol if what Miller (1989) suggests—that the "positive regard or acceptance of failure has no place in public and must be relegated to shadow"

(p. 126)—perverts the symbol's original "raising funds" function into a "profit motive" function, a caricature of itself disconnected from nonviolent direct action, from specific social injustices, or from meaningful statements of social action? Further still, how might depth psychology make sense of the fact that while most of us today still recognize and attach the meaning of *peace* to the symbol, that most of us also have no idea that the simultaneously circular and forked symbol originally represented a "human being in despair?" (Holtom, 1961, p. 6).

In his writings, Jung addresses the implications of a symbol's disconnection from its context on the enantiodromian nature of a symbol's energy/libido, thereby offering possible responses to this question. In Volume 5 of the *Collected Works, Symbols of Transformation*, Jung (1952/1956) suggests that images considered numinous or sacred pick up on the suggestive power of the environment, pointing then toward a bi-directional exchange of energy in that the numinosity of the image imbues its environment, which then "intensifies it in turn" (p. 157 [*CW* 5, para. 223]). In the same way, if the environment does not offer suggestive power to the symbol, then the

> collective effect of the image will be negligible, or nonexistent, even though it may be extremely intense as an individual experience. I mention this circumstance because it is a controversial point whether the inner images, or collective representations, are merely suggested by the environment, or whether they are genuine and spontaneous experiences. The first view simply begs the question, because it is obvious that the content suggested must have come into existence somehow and at some time.
> (p. 157 [*CW* 5, para. 223])

The considerations put forth by Jung also concern the current status of the peace symbol. It surely began as an inner image for Gerald Holtom of a "human being in despair" (1961, p. 6) that unpredictably grew into a larger collective representation of survival, protest, defiance, and resistance. However, its proliferation from an individual's inner image into a collective symbol would not have happened without the assistance of its active, largely attended, nonviolent direct action march environment.

The environment fueled the symbol's energy and presence, and in turn, the symbol intensified the affect and energy of the gathered crowds. Through kairos, the peace symbol and the ND and peace movements became reciprocating fields of energy that propagated the movements, their agendas, and their symbol forward.

However, as the peace symbol became increasingly popular and profitable in mainstream marketing, advertising, and consumerism, its function as determined by those who used it seems to revert it back to that of a *sign*—more or less defined as "a conventional mark, device, or symbol, used technically ... in place of words or names written in ordinary letters" (Sign, n.d.). In these growing numbers of instances, the symbol seems to be "interpreted reductively" (Jung, 1948/1960b, p. 46), requiring that it discard its original meaning of *despair* and only asking of it to take the place of the word or general idea of *peace*. In these commodified contexts, the peace symbol no longer stands for active protest, active defiance, or active resistance in sites of suffering or struggle. Jung would argue that when this shift from three-dimensional fluidity to two-dimensional fixity happens, that it "ignores the real nature of a symbol and debases it into a mere sign" (p. 46). Pinning down a "uniformity of meaning ... toward a fixed significance of symbols" (Jung, 1948/1960a, p. 246) "serves to bind the movement of psychic energy" (Aziz, 1990, p. 16) so that the symbol's psychic energy becomes inflexible. The supple and enantiodromian nature of the symbol then loses its ability to reverberate and resonate, to respond to the needs and desires of the interpreter/viewer, and the energy and its archetypal meaning eventually recede or regress. Finally, in *Archetypes and the Collective Unconscious* (1954/1959), Jung states that "lovely, mysterious, richly intuitive" images can stiffen into "mere objects" and that the "more familiar we are with them the more does constant usage polish them smoothly, so that what remains is only banal superficiality and meaningless paradox" (p. 8). With respect to the peace symbol, these considerations have merit.

The golden shadow theory likewise provides some insights on this question. Nowadays, the peace symbol is commercially ubiquitous. Especially during eras of war, the peace symbol's countermessage readily sells. And because of its graphic simplicity and ability to translate in every color of the rainbow, it is emblazoned on all sorts of products in all sorts of sizes. Since the symbol is unrestricted and entrenched within the public domain, we probably could not smite it out even if we tried. Thus, the peace symbol's presence is simply unavoidable. Perhaps then, in the late 1960s and into the 1970s, when failure to get out of Vietnam was apparent, when failure to reduce nuclear proliferation was evident, when failure to address certain social injustices at home was palpable, it was difficult to not be reminded of these multiple failures with the peace symbol's omnipresence. There was no keeping it out of sight, there was no avoiding it at all costs, there was no way to remove it from national and local discourses and stuff it into the shadow. The culture could not simply shut the symbol in its psychological shadow and hope that it would slowly wither away.

However, whenever the symbol was shined up and positioned in the types of contexts that gave it its original meaning and power—sites of nonviolent and direct action—it retained its ineffable quality and power. Therefore, one way to lessen the cultural wounds of failure might have been to exploit the symbol into ubiquity for capitalistic purposes,[1] stripping it of its meaning and powerful context, desensitizing its viewers, and creating consumers. In this de-contextualized and overexposed state, the ability of the symbol to represent collective affect and possibility becomes a moot point. Its ability instead becomes a question of goods and inventory, profit and loss reports, and consequently, the deeper meaning of the "human being in despair" is discarded and all but disappears. Thus, around its edges, the symbol seems to have atrophied over the years as cultural hegemony works hard to forget, mute, or erase the sites and artifacts of historical and contemporary counter voices and ideas; in other words, the very things it desires would return to the depths of shadow.

And yet, like the fatigued marcher who is dedicated to the cause and keeps putting one foot in front of the other, whether rain or shine, the peace symbol tirelessly shows up for individuals, groups, or situations that call upon its assistance. It is precisely the fluid ability of the peace symbol to be a meaning-full interface that keeps it breathing, functioning, and blooming in sites of struggle and suffering.

Note

1 The U.S. knows the tactic of exploiting the undesirable well—as the histories of Native Americans, Women, the Working Poor, African Americans, Asian Americans, Latino Americans, legal and illegal Immigrants, and numerous other groups outside of mainstream U.S. identities corroborate.

References

Aziz, R. (1990). *C. G. Jung's psychology of religion and synchronicity*. Albany, NY: State University of New York Press.

Campaign for Nuclear Disarmament, (n.d.). The CND symbol. Retrieved from https://cnduk.org/the-symbol/

Duff, P. (1971). *Left, left, left: A personal account of six protest campaigns 1945–1965*. London: Allison & Busby.

Earl, J., Soule, S. A., & McCarthy, J. D. (2003). Protest under fire? Explaining the policing of protest. *American Sociological Review, 68* (4), 581–606.

Hillman, J. (1975). *Revisioning psychology*. New York, NY: Harper and Row.

Holtom, G. (1961, June 2). The ND symbol. *Peace News: The International Pacifist Weekly*, p. 6.

Jung, C. G. (1956). The transformation of the libido (R. F. C. Hull, Trans.) In H. Read et al. (Series Eds.), *The collected works of C. G. Jung* (Vol. 5, pp. 142–170). Princeton, NJ: Bollingen/Princeton University Press. (Original work published 1952).

Jung, C. G. (1959). Archetypes of the collective unconscious (R. F. C. Hull, Trans.) In H. Read et al. (Series Eds.), *The collected works of C. G. Jung* (Vol. 9i, pp. 3–41). Princeton, NJ: Bollingen/Princeton University Press. (Original work published 1954)

Jung, C. G. (1960a). General aspects of dream psychology (R. F. C. Hull, Trans.) In H. Read et al. (Series Eds.), *The collected works of C. G. Jung* (Vol. 8, pp. 237–280). Princeton, NJ: Bollingen/Princeton University Press. (Original work published 1948)

Jung, C. G. (1960b). On psychic energy (R. F. C. Hull, Trans.) In H. Read et al. (Series Eds.), *The collected works of C. G. Jung* (Vol. 8, pp. 1–66). Princeton, NJ: Bollingen/Princeton University Press. (Original work published 1948)

May, R. (1962). The breakdown of symbols. *Dialogue, 2*(4), 3–6.

Meador, B. (2000). The feminine and politics. In T. Singer (Ed.), *The vision thing: Myth, politics and psyche in the world* (pp. 50–61). New York, NY: Routledge.

Miller, W. A. (1989). *Your golden shadow: Discovering and fulfilling your undeveloped self.* San Francisco, CA: Harper & Row.

Rigby, A. (1986). Peace News, 1936–1986. In G. Chester & A. Rigby (Eds.), *Articles of peace: Celebrating fifty years of Peace News* (pp. 7–26). Bridport: Prism Press.

Sign. (n.d.). In *Oxford English dictionary online.* Retrieved from www-oed-com.ezproxy.rollins.edu/view/Entry/179512

Van Eenwyk, J. R. (1997). *Archetypes and strange attractors: The chaotic world of symbols.* Toronto: Inner City Books.

Index

Note: Page numbers in *italic* refers to Tables.

Abrams, J. 14, 40, 82
aestheticization 42–3
alchemy 21–2, 93
Aldermaston March (1958) 52, 55, 56–7, 58, 60–3, 73, 74–6, 90, 92, 93, 95, 111–12, 118, 121
Andriano, J. D. 44–5
apocalypse 21, 26–7, 70, 81
archetypes 18–19, 20–1, 22, 25
atomic age 32, 35–7, 70
Atomic Energy Commission (AEC) 101
Atomic Weapons Establishment (AWE) 54
Austen, Eric 97
Axis Powers 26, 53

brand-images 65, 66
Britain 17, 37, 48, 53, 54–63, 73–6, 77, 87, 92
Brock, Hugh 58–9

Campaign for Nuclear Disarmament (CND) 19, 49, 70, 120; formation and goals 55–6, 60, 90, 119; marches 60–3, 73–6, 91, 92; use of the peace sign 46, 48, 52, 58, 61, 63, 71, 73–4, 75–6, 90–2, 93–5, 118, 122; *see also* Aldermaston March; Peace Movement
Canada 17, 102
chronos 9, 74, 92

Churchill, Winston 53
circular imagery 45–6, 48–9, 68–73, 83, 92, 123
Civil Rights movement 87, 97, 102
Cold War 41–3, 54
collective consciousness 40–1, 48–9; emotions 86–7
colonialism 20, 44
Committee for Nonviolent Action (CNVA) 74, 88, 100–4, 105–6, 107–11, 112–13, 120

Dante Alighieri, *The Divine Comedy* 33–4
depth psychology: history and definition 1–2; use of literature 12–13; views of peace 4–5
Direct Action Committee Against Nuclear War (DAC) 52, 55, 56, 57, 74, 120
draft cards 104–6
Duck and Cover (film, 1951) 22, 41–3
Duff, Peggy 55–6, 63, 67, 75, 90–1, 94–5, 96, 99, 121
Dwight, J. S. 40

Easter, symbolism of 74–5, 92
Edinger, Edward 21
ego 23; American 39, 40, 41, 81; and self 69; and the shadow 13–14, 23, 24–5, 35, 88
Einstein, Albert 16–17, 26, 53
Eisenhower, Dwight D. 39

Index 129

Ellenberger, H. F. 1
emblems 64, 65–6
enantiodromia 9, 28–9, 32–5, 81–2, 84–5, 89, 118, 120; symbols 48–9, 67, 68, 83, 123, 124
Enola Gay (aircraft) 28, 40
extraversion 119–20

fallout shelter sign 45–6, 47–8, 68, 70
Federal Civil Defense Administration (FCDA) 41, 42, 46, 47
figure-ground illusion 85
Frame, Paul 46–7
France 37
Franck Report, The (1945) 27–8
Freud, Sigmund 1, 5–6, 12
frontier myth 20–1
fundraising 4, 90, 113–15
Fussell, Paul 39–40

gay rights movement 87–8, 97
Geddes, Donald P. 35, 36–7
Giegerich, Wolfgang 22, 23, 34, 35, 39
Godzilla: King of the Monsters (film, 1956) 32, 44, 45
Gojira (film, 1954) 22, 44, 54, 86
golden shadow 82–5, 86–90, 92, 93, 95, 96, 118, 119–21
Goya, Francisco: *Sad Presentiments of What Must Come to Pass* 59–60, *62*; *Third of May 1808* 59, *61*
Groves, Leslie R. 20, 23–5, 27

Hillman, James 2, 19, 26, 33, 68, 71, 121
Hiroshima bomb (1945) 7, 28, 35, 37, 39, 44, 46, 48, 54, 77
Hollywood films 40, 43, 44, 45
Holtom, Gerald 56–7, 61, 63, 74–5; design of the peace symbol 57–60, 65, 69–70, 76, 91, 93, 96–7, 99, 118–19, 123
Hopcke, R. H. 14

icons 64, 65

images 64, 65
Inanna-Ishtar (goddess) 34
insignias 65, 66
interconnectedness 3, 87
interdependence 25, 34, 35, 48, 83, 84–5, 91

Japan 63, 77; atomic bombings 7, 28, 35, 37, 38, 39, 41, 44, 46, 48, 54, 77; battle flag 47; mythology 22, 44, 45
Jekyll and Hyde archetype 25
Johnson, Lyndon B. 104–5
Jung, Carl G. 2, 5; archetype concept 18, 25; enantiodromia concept 33; on rebirth symbolism 93; on the shadow 12, 13, 14, 67–8, 82, 88; on symbols 46, 48, 67, 68, 69–71, 77–8; on UFOs 45, 46

kairos 55, 74, 89–90, 92, 95, 96, 118, 124
Kelly, C. C. 16, 23, 24, 27, 28
Kimbles, S. L. 14
Kolsbun, K. 54, 56, 62–3, 74–5
Kramer, M. 36

logos 64, 66
"lollypops" (CND) 58, *59*, 61, 75, 92, 102, 106, 110, 115
Lorenz, H. 41
Los Alamos Laboratory 23, 35

mandalas 46, 48, 68, 69, 70, 71, 83, 92, 93
Manhattan Project (MED) 7, 15–19, 20–2, 23–4, 25, 35, 68; secrecy 25–8, 53–4, 70
Manifest Destiny 19–20
May, Rollo 55, 118, 121
McCarthyism 39
Meador, B. 119, 120
Mercurius (fictional character) 22–3, 39
Miles, B. 6, 59
Miller, William 9, 25, 82–3, 86, 88, 89, 90, 96, 119–20, 122–3

Index

Morley, F. 28, 40
Moss, Norman 62–3

Nagasaki bombing (1945) 7, 28, 35, 37, 39, 44, 46, 48, 54, 77
National Committee for a Sane Nuclear Policy (SANE) 88
ND symbol *see* peace symbol
Newtonian paradigm 84
Nhat Hanh, T. 84
Nichols, Kenneth 24–5
nuclear arms race 16, 23, 41, 54
nuclear physics, archetypal aspects 19–23
nuclear proliferation 37, 77, 119, 122, 125
nuclear weapons: bombings 7, 28, 35, 37, 39, 41, 44, 46, 48, 54, 77; development of 15–18, 20, 23–7, 35–7; justifications for using 39–40; Oppenheimer on 38, 39; religious resistance to 61–2; scientific resistance to 27, 61; *see also* Manhattan Project
nuclear weapons testing 6, 35, 37, 44, 54, 55, 58; resistance to 54–5, 98, 100, 101

olive branch symbol 7, 63, 71, 73
Oppenheimer, J. Robert 20, 23, 35, 38–9
opposites: binary 4–5, 34–5; symbolism 68–71, 76, 84, 92–3
origami crane symbol 63
Ostergaard, G. 55

patriarchal power structures 34, 86
Pax Cultura symbol 71–2
peace: binary opposition to war 4–5, 35; representations of 3–5
Peace Movement 19, 81–2; and the golden shadow 120–1; sense of failure 122–3, 125; use of the peace symbol 118–19; *see also* Campaign for Nuclear Disarmament
peace symbol (ND symbol): advocating for a position 97, 103–6; commercial use and misuse 7, 122, 124–5; demonstrating direct action-in-the-moment 97, 100–2; design 1, *2*, 57–60, 65, 69–70, 76, 91, 93, 96–7, 99, 118–19, 123; drawing attention to issues 97, 102, *103*; emergence 46, 48, 78; indicating available resources 97, 111–13; raising funds 90, 97, 113–15; recruitment 97, 106–7; requesting future action 97, 98–100; as research subject 6–7; significance to the Peace Movement 83, 93–5, 115, 118–19, 121–4, 125; supporting activism 97, 107–9; as symbol 66–7, 68–71, 72–6, 77, 78; transcending local languages 97, 110–11; use by CND 46, 48, 52, 58, 61, 63, 71, 73–4, 75–6, 90–2, 93–5, 118, 122; as visual device 63–4, 65–6
peace symbols, historical 7, 63, 71, 73, 93
Pearl Harbor attack (1941) 20
percepticide 41
Perera, Sylvia Brinton 34, 35
Petition to the President of the United States, A (1945) 27–8
Prometheus myth 28, 37–9, 77, 81
propaganda 39–40
public imaginary 40–1, 43, 44–5, 85–6

quaternity 68, 70–1

radiation 37, 42, 54; warning signs 45–8, 68, 73
radioactive psyche 32, 37, 41–9, 67, 68, 70, 72–3, 77, 97
rainbow symbol 63, 71, 73
Randle, Michael 52, 55, 56, 91
rebirth 70, 74, 76, 92, 93
Rigby, Andrew 119, 121
Roerich Pact movement 71–2
Romanyshyn, R. D. 33

Roosevelt, Franklin D. 16–17, 26, 27, 53
Rosenthal, P. 71

Samuels, A. 13–14, 33
Schweber, S. S. 15, 38
science fiction 41, 43, 45, 70, 83
self: archetype 18–19; and ego 69
semaphore 65, *66*, 75, 90, 91, 96
shadow: American 39, 40, 41, 81; cleavage 67–8; and the ego 13–14, 23, 24–5, 35, 88; and the golden shadow 82–5, 86–90, 92, 93, 95, 96, 118, 119–21; in literature 12–13; projection 14, 44–5
signs 64, 65
Singer, T. 14
social inertia 88–9
social justice issues 3, 102, 121–2
Soviet Union 28, 37, 41, 55
Spirit of Freedom, The (boat) 107–8
Stein, M. 14
Stevens, A. 14
strategic structural change 96
Student Peace Union (SPU) 88, 98, 102, 112, 120
symbols: definition 65, 66–7; function 118

Tarnas, R. 6
Telephone War Tax Refusal Campaign 103–4, *105*
television programs 43, 85–6

Tims, Margaret 69, 75–6, 92
Truman, Harry S. 27, 28, 39

UFOs 32, 45, 68, 70, 86
Unilateral Nuclear Disarmament (UND) 60, 66, 73, 97, 102, 108
uroborus *33*, 120

Van Eenwyk, J. R. 8, 18, 33, 73, 77, 94, 119
Vietnam War 9, 125
visual devices, types of 63–5
Von Franz, Marie-Louise 2, 6, 71, 91

war, binary opposition to peace 4–5, 35
War of the Worlds (radio drama) 7, 21
War Resisters League 73
Watkins, M. 41
Welles, Orson 7, 21
Wendt, Gerald 35, 36–7
white dove symbol 7, 63, 71, 73
women's movement 87, 97
World War II (WWII) 7, 12, 14–18, 19, 20, 21, 23–8; atomic bombings 7, 28, 35, 37, 38, 39, 41, 44, 46, 48, 54, 77
World War I (WWI) 21

Yin-Yang symbol 83–4

Zeus (god) 38, 39
Zweig, C. 14, 40, 82

Taylor & Francis eBooks

www.taylorfrancis.com

A single destination for eBooks from Taylor & Francis with increased functionality and an improved user experience to meet the needs of our customers.

90,000+ eBooks of award-winning academic content in Humanities, Social Science, Science, Technology, Engineering, and Medical written by a global network of editors and authors.

TAYLOR & FRANCIS EBOOKS OFFERS:

- A streamlined experience for our library customers
- A single point of discovery for all of our eBook content
- Improved search and discovery of content at both book and chapter level

REQUEST A FREE TRIAL
support@taylorfrancis.com

For Product Safety Concerns and Information please contact our EU representative GPSR@taylorandfrancis.com
Taylor & Francis Verlag GmbH, Kaufingerstraße 24, 80331 München, Germany

www.ingramcontent.com/pod-product-compliance
Lightning Source LLC
Chambersburg PA
CBHW051751230426
43670CB00012B/2239